Feb 2010

The Pineapple Dance Book

To dear Kaori!
Keep on dancing's
love
Debbie

The PINEAPPLE DANCE BOOK

presented by Debbie Moore

An Insider's Guide to All That's Best
in Dance and Exercise Today

Text by Gay Search and David Roper

PAVILION
MICHAEL JOSEPH

I know that all my wonderful family and friends
will understand that I wish to dedicate this book to
Doctor Chandra Sharma

First published in Great Britain in 1983 by
Pavilion Books Limited
192 Shaftesbury Avenue, London WC2H 8JL
In association with Michael Joseph Limited
44 Bedford Square, London WC1B 3DU

Designed by Bernard Higton

Moore, Debbie
    The Pineapple dance book.
    1. Dancing
    I. Title
    793.3   GV1594
    ISBN 0-907516-28-9

Printed in Italy by New Interlitho

CONTENTS

Foreword by Wayne Sleep

FOREWORD

by Wayne Sleep

Dance has been my life since I was twelve years old, so it has been really exciting for me to witness the current dance boom, with thousands of people of all ages getting the same sort of pleasure from it as I do, taking classes in tap or jazz or contemporary for their own sake, as well as for keeping fit.

And there's no doubt that dance is a great way of keeping fit. It keeps you young (we hope!), it gets your body working at its best with your muscles in tune, and it's a great feeling, knowing that your body can do anything you want it to do.

Doing class every day is part of my life – like cleaning my teeth. I feel really bad if I miss it and I get irritable because I haven't stretched my body out properly. The first thing cats do when they wake up is have a really good stretch, and we need to do the same. The only difference is that it takes them thirty seconds, and it takes us an hour and a half!

The bonus you get from dance as a career is that you're keeping fit while you're earning your living – being a dancer means you never have to work out after work! It's also a great way of getting rid of tension and aggression, and like yoga, it leaves you feeling at peace with yourself.

Another benefit of the dance boom and the growth of centres like Pineapple is that amateurs and professionals are together under the same roof. It's good for amateurs because they can watch professionals working out and can see what they're aiming at, and it's good for us because it's creating a much wider and more knowledgeable audience for dance. If people come along to a show – which they might not have done before – and see us doing something they've tried in class, they know just how difficult it is, and so they're more appreciative.

Just one word of caution. As a result of the dance boom, a lot of unqualified people, with no knowledge of anatomy, are setting up as teachers, and if people go to their classes, they run the risk of injuring themselves.

So, make sure that your teacher is well qualified, and get dancing!

Wayne Sleep
April 1983

Pineapple...the first slice

Dancing as a way to stay fit and healthy has everything going for it! People think that I am either a retired dancer, or else that I spend a large part of my day teaching some of the many thousands who pass through Pineapple's doors. In fact, nothing could be further from the truth . . . although there's certainly the odd childhood dream hidden away there. But, if I didn't grow up to fulfil some of those childhood ambitions, I think I have done the next best thing. And I hope you agree as you come to meet just a few of the many famous faces and teachers who are our friends, and who will introduce you to all the exciting ways to get the most out of dance, perhaps capturing a part of the excitement that has made Pineapple the extraordinary centre that it is today.

My connection with dance goes back quite some time, well before the idea for a Pineapple had even materialised. Already a successful fashion model, I began inexplicably, so it seemed then, to suffer from a condition known as 'hypo-thyroid' (the opposite of 'hyper-thyroid', where the thyroid gland is overactive). I watched in horror as my weight ballooned up from around eight stone to way over eleven.

Anyone who has ever been struck by it knows what I mean when I say that the outcome is all too real . . . and apparent! And added to this was the possible loss of everything I had achieved in my career to date. No one wants a size eight model suddenly turning up for a session wearing a size fourteen!

There followed what seemed like an endless round of doctors' waiting-rooms and consultations with specialists in conventional medicine, all apparently conspiring to give me no hope whatever. Advice ranged from 'an incurable condition' to 'you will lose weight as soon as you stop eating'! Since I was barely eating anyway, you can imagine how I raged inside at what seemed like either hopeless indifference or downright callousness.

My husband Norris insists that only my dogged persistence eventually led me to look at more 'unconventional' forms of medicine, though I maintain it was just a stroke of luck. However it came about, my meeting with a homeopathic doctor not only gave me *hope* (the essential ingredient of any cure) but also unwittingly influenced my entire future when he recommended dance as an ideal exercise programme alongside his homeopathic remedies. And this was long before dance had undergone the boom of recent years.

I have never been fanatical about anything, but I think it's worth mentioning that the effect of my doctor's 'cure' together with his constantly sought and given advice over the years has totally changed the way I think and feel about my body, the things I eat, and my overall lifestyle. I am not averse to the odd bit of 'junk' food every once in a while – I'm sure it gives you a sense of balance – but I would never eat such food on a daily basis. Let's face it: much of it *is* pure poison, and there can't be many people around who haven't been enlightened by the enormous number of articles and the massive media coverage there is on the subject of 'we are what we eat'.

Homeopathy has taught me to be aware of my body and its needs, to care for it as a gardener cares for and nourishes his garden. You must know it well enough to see its weak spots and respond. Ten years on I am completely cured and my entire lifestyle has changed. Part of that change has meant an involvement with dance – to a degree I would never have imagined possible.

Hot on the heels of my doctor's advice I took myself off to a dance studio, the only place in Lodon you could go at the time to find really excellent classes. Imagine everyone's surprise, not to say *panic*, when its owners suddenly decided to close down. I wasn't the only wife who had driven her husband mad by leaving the house three nights a week to do her own thing. And on top of that there were some forty-five teachers and almost the entire dance population of London out on the streets without a home. . .

My immediate thought was to get up a petition and force them to re-open, though this would come to nothing. Then, with thoughts already on my future plans once the modelling days were over, I found myself with a real mission in life. I would open my own studios! At the time it all seemed like such a good idea. If anyone tried to make me see reason (and Norris did try) there I was with some blind faith and a thoroughly convincing argument: that I *would* find the right building, that I *would* one day fill it

with dancers, and that I *would* make it a success. I'm still not clear who I was trying to reassure the most.

Like all the best laid plans, if I could have imagined the obstacles and constant difficulties that were to present themselves, I might have had second thoughts. Needless to say, I am glad I didn't. I like to think that everything associated with dance and Pineapple has benefited in a way that was only a dream four years ago, when I chanced upon a disused pineapple warehouse in Covent Garden.

Convincing a sympathetic bank manager, mortgaging the house and putting in everything I had saved from my modelling days were the risks I was prepared to take. Endless problems with builders, surveyors, fire officers, health inspectors, etc., followed, and at first we even guaranteed that membership fees would be refunded if people didn't like Pineapple. Our fears proved to be groundless, though, and at the time of writing, our membership numbers over thirty thousand. But it hasn't all been so easy.

Planting the seeds...

At the age of fifteen – like most young girls, I imagine – I just couldn't wait to leave school and get out into the real world. I just wanted to be out there exploring, meeting people and letting life happen.

My opportunity came without warning when I was entered for a modelling competition in a local store in my home town of Manchester. Like all the best stories, I won, and the prize was £25 with a course at a modelling school. Even more unexpectedly came an assignment, some months later, for *Honey* magazine . . . to model for them in New York. From then on it seemed there was no looking back.

By the time I was eighteen (much too young!) I was married to one of Manchester's top fashion photographers, and about to settle down to what looked like the ideal life. We were even featured in a television documentary called 'Model Couple' as 'the Shrimpton and Bailey of the north'. Until one day he left for an assignment and didn't bother to come home. I was only just twenty.

A year later I had filed for divorce, packed my bags and, with my parents' blessing, come to London, as much to start a new career as to escape the reminders of the past. But that kind of hurt never disappears without trace, and while I was soon working with the best photographers, my body was not so ready for the massive changes I was so eager to make. Since then my doctor has explained to me how the hypo-thyroid condition I was to suffer from for so long was in fact a direct result not only of the

At the height of my modelling career and (below) that wonderful New York trip that started it all

psychological blow caused by my marriage breaking up, but years of poor diet and lack of exercise. Because I was always slim I had never felt it necessary to get involved in diet or exercise programmes.

Articles and programmes that tackle the problems of a body reacting to stress and mental trauma really interest me. For me, dancing is such an enormous plus in helping not only to be ready for these moments, which seem to strike most of us, but also to get us over those hurdles more efficiently and safely. We all know what it's like to want to have a good cry, but how many times do we feel we either mustn't or shouldn't? That's something very similar, and dancing can be the most marvellous relief. Honestly, I can't recommend it highly enough!

Watching them grow...

So, four years after we opened in Covent Garden, there is already a second Pineapple – Pineapple West – close to the heart of the West End. The large ground floor studio has been host to a number of television, stage and film productions, including 'Cats', 'Song and Dance' and 'Nutcracker' with Joan Collins – not forgetting the Kids from Fame who invaded us last Christmas and treated us to one memorable rehearsal.

Also in that time we have expanded to become a public company, something which gives not only ourselves, but dance as a whole, genuine credibility.

The big day – launching Pineapple at the Stock Exchange and (right) relaxing with Wayne Sleep

It enables us to put into action our plans for growth throughout Britain as well as allowing us to build a 'bridge' for dance across the nations and provide a home for everyone who believes, as we do, that dancing is for everyone!

As you read through the book and get to meet some of our teachers, and eventually find your way to the special classes they have devised for you to do at home, I hope you begin to learn some of the answers to the questions we are frequently asked about dance and exercise today. To help you further, I have set down *ten* rules at the start of that section which I think are applicable to everyone and which should be borne in mind by anyone who wants to pursue a dance/exercise programme. I hope you find them useful.

Lastly, I would like to thank the people who have made this first book possible and without whom Pineapple would not be what it is today. They are: David, who runs the Pineapple Agency and supplies dancers for major productions throughout the world; Becky, who somehow manages to organise some 400 classes in both centres week after week, keeping over 150 teachers (not to mention the staff and the members!) sane and happy; Richard and Danka, who run the largest dancewear shop in Europe together with two other retail outlets and a vast wholesale department; all the staff; Micky and his boys for finally solving our building problems; many of the teachers, including Arlene, John, Charles, Kay, Sandy, Michael, Sylvia, Maryon and everyone else who gave of their time so generously. I also have to thank Jeremy Enness for taking the bulk of the photographs; Rupert for his knitwear design especially for the book; Andrew, of Andrew Lockyer Ltd for everybody's hair; Steven, our artistic director who played a major role in every part of the preparation of this book; Colin Webb at Pavilion Books who had the foresight to suggest this book and who has supported it unreservedly; Judy Dauncey, the editor, Bernard Higton, the art director; David Roper and Gay Search, who made sense of all the information we gave them; not forgetting Yve; my daughter Lara; and last but not least my husband Norris, without whom none of this would have been possible.

Debbie Moore
April 1983

From the Pineapple scrapbook...

In the beginning... there was just a pineapple warehouse

Becky keeps the timetables (and us!) in order

Now the choice is yours

It can be a great spectator sport too!

Crowded corridors before classes begin

Invaded by beauty...Miss Brazil, Miss Switzerland and Miss Denmark work out at Pineapple before the Miss World contest

Shooting location scenes for 'Nutcracker' the film that starred Joan Collins, Finola Hughes and lots of our students!

Part 1

INSIDE PINEAPPLE

In this section, we look at the main areas of dance and how they are taught at Pineapple. Our teachers tell you what makes each style so special, and what you can expect if you join a dance class. There is just so much to learn about dance that we *could* write a book on each style, but here we have outlined the basics, to enable you to make your own choice. And for those who want to probe a little deeper, we have some suggestions on how to find out more.

Where It All Began

Like many women, when I was a child I used to dream of being a ballerina, of pirouetting in a tutu in front of the world. I hardly aspired to be the next Fonteyn, but I did want to dance. Life, it seems, had other plans! Here at Pineapple, though, it doesn't matter if dancing passed you by the first time around, because our beginners classes are for beginners of any age, and a lot of us go to ballet classes for the sheer pleasure of it, not in order to become ballerinas. And we're especially proud to have as one of our teachers Maryon Lane (right), a principal ballerina with the Royal Ballet for many years, who is living proof – if anyone is – that dancing keeps you young!

Just after one of her packed classes for professional dancers, Maryon and I had tea in the Pineapple café, and I was able to talk to her about her career and why people still dream of the stage . . . despite all the hard work and disappointments. A dancer's working life is often shorter than a professional footballer's, and few make it to the stature of Fonteyn, Nureyev or Baryshnikov.

'Ballet seems to be more popular than ever at the moment,' she told me. 'And we're attracting more and more boys these days, but it is a shame that so many of them come to ballet late. They start at anything from seventeen to twenty. But one of the boys told me the other day how they might go to a discothèque and see one guy doing some amazingly intricate, fascinating footwork, and they discover that he's had dance training. And it's funny, but this can be the thing that starts them off. Of course, if they start earlier it's easier – on the mind as well as the body – because there's so much to take in. Still, I've seen excellent dancers who started really late come out on top: it just means a much more condensed type of course and taking a much more dedicated attitude to it all.'

Maryon began dancing at what she calls the 'ridiculously early' age of three and a half, when she had to learn everything, like tap, Greek dancing and Spanish dancing, which she now sees was a perfect background from which to work. Tap she particularly likes, and is pleased that it's now very much back in vogue, because 'you learn rhythm, style and music, it's lovely!'

One thing that has always puzzled me is why ballet classes are conducted in French, so I asked Maryon if she could explain to me how it came about.

'Ballet originally started in France, in Louis XIV's court (the word "bal" means a ball or dance, so "ballet" means a little dance), so basic steps were called out in French. Just as we traditionally

associate the opera with Italy, so the home of ballet is France, and that has its advantages. For instance, if I travel, then I can go to Japan, say, and they might not understand a word of English, but they'll know exactly what step I mean . . . it's an international language in that way. Strange, isn't it, one just accepts the fact that it's in French, you know.'

And are they the same steps as those that were danced in the French court?

'Ballet has a tradition of about five centuries now,

BALLET

A form of theatrical entertainment contained within a strict academic school, marrying dance with the various talents of music and design. Ballet classes always start at the 'barre', which supports the balance of the body while it completes various routines designed to increase strength, mobility and 'turn out' (a rotation of the entire leg outwards from the hip joint, giving the distinctive 'classical line' associated with ballet and enabling the body to balance more efficiently).

Benefits

The discipline required develops a heightened sense of grace and fluidity. Based on a very correct alignment of the body, it can be intensely satisfying and enjoyable to pursue, gradually strengthening and altering the body shape after many years of work.

Further Reading

Cyril W. Beaumont: *Complete Book of Ballets* (Putnam)
Peter Brinson and Clement Crisp: *Ballet for All* (Pan Books)
Mary Clarke and David Vaughan (editors): *Encyclopaedia of Dance and Ballet* (Pitman Publishing)
Francis Coleman: *Bluff Your Way into Ballet* (Wolf Publishing Ltd)
Joyce Mackie: *Basic Ballet* (W. Russell Turner)

Maryon Lane, as she appeared as a principal dancer with the Royal Ballet

One of the world's leading male dancers, Mikhail Baryshnikov (right), recreating the title role of 'Le Spectre de la Rose', first danced by Nijinsky in 1911

and although it's a strict dance technique it has evolved to a degree. After all, in those early days they were heavily weighed down by their dress and influenced by etiquette, and obviously that determined the way they moved. As society became more tolerant, and more than just a glimpse of ankle was permitted on stage, *and* methods of training the body were being refined, so a more extensive technique could develop. No longer restrained by costumes, dancers were able to leave the ground and ''spin'' more easily.

'Of course, even today that technique is changing subtly under the influence of contemporary dancers and choreographers. But it all takes place within the confines of a strict academic school. Having been brought up in the Royal Ballet with people like Ninette de Valois and Frederick Ashton, and teachers like Vera Volkova, I inherited a very pure style, handed down from the court to the present day. And in my own teaching I am very concerned with those things: purity and a correctness of detail.'

So, what would Maryon recommend to somebody who suddenly decides they have to dance?

'Start at a good school: a good teacher is *very* important. Ideally children should start at about the age of eight. If they're taught well and they're keen, then they should eat sensibly and keep slim for their career's sake. If you want to start at sixteen or seventeen, then go to a very good beginners' class and just see how you get on. If you like it, you're going to work hard and take care that you look good. But if you're just not up to it, then I know it can be heartbreaking. Ballet is a terribly hard career in that sense. Most dancers under-rate themselves anyway. People walk away to the side of the class and sulk, and I remember being furious with myself when I couldn't manage this or that. Sometimes even the very best dancers are upset with themselves, and then I think: what a shame they don't see just how good they are. One does one's best to try and tell them. For those who aren't so good, they need a close friend to say to them: "Look, take it up as a hobby, do it for pleasure, but you are not going to make it professionally." It has become harder and harder to get into a company, so if somebody's honest with you, it can be a help.'

Basic Ballet

Exercises at the barre are a vital part of ballet training, and here we show three basic exercises which you could try at home by following the instructions very carefully. Pliés are of fundamental importance in any study of classical ballet. The port de bras is a warm-up exercise that increases flexibility of the spine, thighs and hamstrings. The battements en cloche loosen the hip and knee joints.

Plié (left)

'Plié' is a French term meaning to bend. It gives pliancy to the legs, and warms and tones the muscles and joints. It prepares the body for further work, and eventually the seemingly effortless nature of jumping that is associated with classical ballet. As an exercise it is performed as one continuous movement.

Starting position: place the hand lightly on the barre or suitable waist-high support. The legs are 'turned-out' with the feet in first position (heels placed together, the toes pointing outwards). Check your spine for correct posture, placing shoulders slightly in front of the pelvis, the pelvis over the heels.

Demi-plié (half-bend): in a correct plié alignment the knees bend out in line with the toes – under no circumstances should you allow them to fold inwards. To achieve a wide turnout, as illustrated, takes time and training. If you cannot keep your knees over your toes, turn your feet in a little more.

Grande plié (full bend): in a full plié the body posture remains the same. In first position the heels come off the floor naturally, but you must ensure your heels are back on the floor as early as possible as you return to the starting position.

Port de bras (right, above)

Standing in first position take the arm above the head and reach forward and out as you bend forwards, eventually placing the forehead on the shin bone. To return, reach out and away, attempting to elongate the body as you bend backwards. The stretches are illustrated by an advanced student, and you should only go as far as it is comfortably possible. Check your posture at all times.

Battements en cloche en attitude (leg swings with a bent knee) (right, below)

Place the working leg behind you with the foot fully stretched. Sweep the leg through first position until it is waist high in front of the body, keeping the knee bent. The height of the swing will be determined by the natural looseness in the hip joint, which should increase with practice. Continue the movement back through first position taking the leg to the back. This exercise should be done without tension of any sort, keeping the hips squarely placed at all times, and with complete stillness of the supporting leg.

Where Will It End?

According to Maryon Lane, there is a big difference between classical ballet and modern dance. Modern dance is an essentially twentieth century phenomenon. The earliest exponents were mostly women, and invariably American. Emancipated from the restraints of the Victorian era, they fought against the formality of the 'danse d'école' (classical ballet), and its often 'trivial' content, seeking instead to establish more clearly their own identity, and ways to communicate what they saw as more 'important' issues. Often without any real formal training they began to devise ways of using the body in a more 'natural', or 'organic' way. As they strove for perfection, many of them evolved their own language and technique by which they came to be known, and laid the foundations for modern dance as we know it today.

Anthony van Laast, currently one of the top all-round choreographers in Britain, and a former soloist with London Contemporary Dance Theatre, says it is that 'earthiness' which is unique to both contemporary and jazz dance. Modern dance exploits gravity, instead of attempting ballet's illusion of transcending it.

Britain probably still lags a generation behind

Martha Graham, undoubtedly one of the most influencial figures in modern dance, in one of the many dances she has choreographed, 'Letter to the World'

America when it comes to contemporary dance and choreography. The first break with tradition can be pinpointed to Isadora Duncan's notions of free movement, which then grew in Germany and America simultaneously. Following that, Ruth St Denis and Ted Shawn, her husband, formed a school and a company in the 1920s in the United States. Out of that company came Martha Graham, and in turn from her company came Merce Cunningham, Paul Taylor and Eric Hawkins, who have already spawned a third generation of movement in the States. Bringing it over to Britain was the responsibility of Robert Cohan, who became

director of the London Contemporary Dance Theatre in 1967.

Anthony is one of the first graduates of that school, along with Siobhan Davies and Micha Bergese. He claims he has no classical training because he realised at an early age: 'I was useless'. But he was still desperate to dance and saw his best option was to study as a contemporary dancer. Now, he in turn teaches, and is adamant that this is one of the most rewarding and most important things any dancer could hope to do.

'There is a common misconception about dance teachers that suggests they are people who never made it, but that is so wrong. All professional dancers have a responsibility to teach so that good young dancers can come through, because when you think about it, a choreographer is only as good as his

MODERN DANCE

Basically a twentieth century phenomenon. It is often associated with freestyle, barefoot dancing, although it invariably masks a highly developed technique.

Benefits

Accessible to a wide age group, it is less restrained than ballet by the requirements of an academic style, and is open to individual interpretation. It strengthens the entire body, particularly the abdomen and lower spine.

Further Reading

Doris Humphries: *The Art of Making Dances* (Dance Books)
Joseph Mazo: *Prime Movers* (Adam and Charles Black)
Don McDonagh: *The Complete Guide to Modern Dance* (Doubleday, New York)
Jan Murray: *Dance Now* (Penguin Books)
John Percival: *Modern Ballet* (Herbert Press Ltd)

Anthony van Laast rehearsing with Finola Hughes, star of 'Cats' and 'Song and Dance'

Lucy Burge of Ballet Rambert dancing 'Five Brahms Waltzes in the Manner of Isadora Duncan', created by Sir Frederick Ashton. Isadora Duncan spearheaded the revolt against the rigid confines of classical ballet in the early years of this century. Modern dance is continuously developing, and Michael Clark, having trained at the Royal Ballet School, is now a leading exponent of the avant-garde.

dancers. And as a choreographer I like my dancers to lend a lot to a new piece. I was a dancer with a company for nine years, but in the end you become just an instrument of someone else's imagination, which is no good for somebody like me who wants to let their own imagination work.'

Before long it looks as though there will be less and less specialisation among dancers and more and more combination of the various different techniques: dancers who can do everything in every field. In this country Wayne Sleep was one of the first (Anthony wrote a ballet for Wayne's show *Dash*, as well as choreographing the entire dance section of *Song and Dance*, which was first performed by Wayne, then by Stephen Jefferies, another classical

dancer from the Royal Ballet.) It doesn't mean that training has to take twice or three times as long: in fact, by doing everything a dancer can achieve a lot more energy and strength.

Modern dance, like classical ballet, is subject to change. In ballet, changes in method and style take place within the context of an academic tradition. Modern dance with its reliance on individuals is more often found in a state of revolt, rather than refinement. Hence there has emerged a whole new generation of 'rebels' under the umbrella of the 'post-moderns', equally bent on continuing the traditions begun by those early pioneers. As barriers break down it is possible we might see the emergence of a new type of dancer and a new type of dancing,

All That Jazz

Everyone seems to think that jazz dancing is a free-form style, where you can just have a good time and do your own thing. But jazz dancing does have certain basic familiar moves. In fact, it is just like ballet in that it is a very specific form with very specific movements, and then variations on those movements. The difference is that every jazz teacher teaches his or her own specific style. Whether it is fast or lyrical, it is highly technical and very high-powered, yet to look at a performer on stage you might think it was the most natural thing in the world.

Jazz dancing is still much bigger in the States than it is in Britain, but that's no surprise when you learn

JAZZ

The kind of energetic dancing often associated with musicals and television spectaculars, and groups such as 'Hot Gossip'. Related to jazz music it has its basis in improvisation on one hand and strict technique on the other.

Benefits

As the requirements of technique and physique are not so exacting for jazz as for classical dancing, it is accessible to almost anyone motivated to dance. Popular open classes are accompanied by extremely lively music which can make this dance style a lot of fun to learn. No less rigorous than any other technique, it strengthens the body, increases speed and co-ordination, and greatly increases suppleness.

Further Reading

Gus Giordano: *Anthology of Jazz Dance Technique* (Orion)
Luigi and Kenneth Wydro: *Luigi Jazz Dance Technique* (Dolphin Books)
Arlene Phillips: *Kiss* (tape, video and booklet) available through Pineapple Mail Order
Marshall and Jean Stearns: *Jazz Dance: The Story of American Vernacular Dance* (Macmillan)
Fred Traguth: *Modern Jazz Dance* (Dance Motion Press)

that it was based on a mixture of African and European dances, and still attracts mostly black performers. It was popularised in America by Jack Cole, who taught Marilyn Monroe everything she knew about dance, and he is regarded as one of the 'soul jazz' dancers. The other kind is 'rock jazz' and at Pineapple you can find both kinds being taught: the first by Charles Augins (though Charles doesn't altogether approve of the two divisions being made) and the second by Arlene Phillips.

The main distinction between the two is the music. Rock jazz is more free-form, like the dances you see Hot Gossip do – the effect is strikingly visual, and the technique is adapted to suit the music. American soul jazz comes from three different techniques, even though it was based on a mixture of modern, ballet, Haitian and West Indian dances. 'He took the turn-out and turned it in!' says Charles, who studied under Jack Cole for a time.

Ballet is ballet around the world. Jazz varies from teacher to teacher, from choreographer to choreographer. It has the feel of American black music, but it has a solid background in ballet. Many people who come to jazz are ballet dancers who want to try something new, because it is truly *new*: a dancer can see a step in a disco, then use it and shape it as a jazz step. A dancer can perform jazz to *any* music . . . sometimes no music at all, sometimes the latest rock or disco sound.

The first jazz music from New Orleans was supposed to make your body start wiggling about, twisting and gyrating to the sound. And all jazz dancing is a bit like that: instead of rules and restrictions you can give way to your own spontaneous vitality, hence it has always been the dance form that is very creative and very personal. It can even be performed without any formal training at all . . . it just 'happens' like the folk dances from where it grew, the bluegrass shuffles of the deep South. Now, the latest form of jazz dancing is the disco dances you see on 'Top of the Pops'. And, of

George Chakiris and Rita Moreno in 'West Side Story'

Hot Gossip in their latest television spectacular, and (below) The Kids from Fame – live on stage in London

course, it was in Arlene's classes at Pineapple that she continued to gather together her best pupils for Hot Gossip, the disco dance group that took England by storm.

Of all the classes I take, I think jazz is my favourite. It's the one which always has really good funky music, it's the one that has a fantastic stretch and bend and floor warm-up at the start of the class, and at the end we are all taught a part of a routine that builds up over several classes into a little section of a dance.

Ever since it began more than fifty years ago, jazz dancing has evolved with whatever music is popular at the time, and some of these are now legendary, like the Charleston and the Jitterbug. So jazz dance is changing every day, which is probably why somebody once said: 'It can be heard, felt and seen, but it is very difficult to define.'

Charles Augins has taught ballet as well as training professionally in both ballet and jazz, and most jazz dancers acknowledge that it is a great advantage to start out with a formal training in either modern dance or ballet, although jazz today is taught and recognised as a form in its own right. When you compare it to ballet you can instantly see the difference: ballet is strict and controlled. Jazz comes from the soul. Or, if you prefer, from the stomach. The jazz-orientated person has to feel the movement starting in the stomach, then passing through the rest of the body like a wave, gently undulating. If you can feel that, that's jazz.

Charles Augins . . . *giving gentle encouragement to his class*

Fancy Footwork

There seem to be two enormous fears that worry men so much that they won't come along to dance classes. The first is the thought of being the only man in the class. And the other is a dread of wearing tights. No man, apart from a professional dancer, will attend a class if he has to wear tights, so Derek Hartley tells everyone to wear loose trousers. That and the keep-fit craze means that he now has some classes where men outnumber women. Or is it because tap-dancing is associated with smooth, suave and sophisticated Fred Astaire walking off into the night with ladies like Ginger Rogers, Cyd Charisse, Rita Hayworth or Mitzi Gaynor? And, more recently, the likes of Princess Di, who has been known to pull on a pair of tap shoes.

Everybody who watches Fred Astaire or Gene Kelly thinks to themselves, 'Wow, that looks easy, I bet I could do that.' Well, it sure looks easy, but you need a sense of rhythm, a sense of jazz music, a good listening ear, an alert brain . . . and fast footwork. What you don't need are strong muscles, long legs or super fitness.

But you might need some patience: Derek reckons it will take most people about a year to learn enough basic steps to begin to establish their own personal style, which is what his particular 'American Tap' concentrates on . . . the really sophisticated Fred Astaire look. But in three months you'll have picked up enough to go home and enjoy yourself. The difference between the English and the American styles is enormous: English style is bouncy and has lots of arm and leg movements. American is based on the original tap dances of the thirties and forties – and keeps the foot and ankle work very close to the floor, giving a smoother, more relaxed look.

Interest in tap dancing has gone in cycles of around thirty years, and the current boom is proof that tap has never been so popular. All the

The inimitable Fred Astaire with Paulette Goddard in 'Second Chorus'; (left) Gene Kelly, unforgettable in 'Singing in the Rain'; and Wayne Sleep and Linda Mae Brewer (right) dazzling today's audiences with their tap-dancing routine from 'Song and Dance'

professional dancers seem to want to widen their repertoire by learning tap. Yet tap has always been essentially a people's or 'popular' dance, sharing as it does a common root with traditional clog dances, Russian step dances and Irish jigs and reels. Still, American tap will always be out on its own – a fusion that comes from the unique amalgam of cultures in the New World. In Britain we never had that jazz tradition belonging to the likes of Count Basie and Duke Ellington, two of the musicians whose music Derek finds ideal for teaching tap dancing.

Once you have mastered steps like wings, pick-ups, cramp-rolls, maxi-fords (named after Max Ford!) time steps, spins, turns and jumps, you can move up within your basic rhythm, letting your imagination run riot and putting in as many steps as imaginatively as you can. It is a combination of speed, control and relaxation perfectly summed up when you watch Fred Astaire, who epitomises European 'carriage' with black American tap style. Gene Kelly, on the other hand, is American new jazz style with black tap. The stage musical *42nd Street* is typical of white American style.

It may sound confusing, but once you have the expertise, you can look – and *sound* – pretty slick.

TAP DANCING

Tap dancing is most generally associated with the films and musicals of Fred Astaire and Gene Kelly. The percussive sounds produced by metal plates on the soles of their shoes tapping out intricate rhythms distinguish this particular dance form.

Benefits

Anybody at any age can have a go. It might fulfil your fantasies, and in a very short space of time give you a real sense of accomplishment. This is a very fun way of staying in shape.

Further Reading

Paul Draper: *On Tap Dancing* (Marcel Dekker Inc.)
Dinan Washbourne: *Basic Tap Dancing* (W. Russell Turner)

Tip Top Tap . . .

Shuffle Ball Step
1 Stand with the feet apart, weight on the left side, the right heel raised with the toe-tap in contact with the floor and the knees slightly bent.

2 Lift the right leg slightly behind and swing forward, from the knee, striking the toe-tap on the floor (Beat 1).

3 Swinging back on the reflex action strike the toe-tap on the floor again – leaving the foot raised (Beat 2)

Heel Pull-back
1 Lift the heels, weight on the balls of both feet.

2 Swinging the right leg forward from the knee, the leg straightens and the back of the heel strikes the floor.

3 and 4 On the reflex action of the leg swinging back, the toe-tap strikes once . . .

Travelling Paddle and Roll
1 Start with the weight over the left foot, the right heel raised, knees bent.

2 Straighten the right leg from the knee and strike the back of the heel on the floor (Beat 1).

3 On the reflex action back from the knee the toe-tap strikes once (Beat 2) leaving the foot raised.

4 Lift the left toe and . . .

5 . . . strike the floor (Beat 3).

6 Bring the feet together, right foot to the left, lowering through the ball of the foot until both feet are flat on the floor. Repeat to the other side.
You should hear *4* toe-tap strikes.
Count: and one and two . . .

5 . . . and then lands on the ball of the foot (that's the pull-back).

6 Prepare to repeat to the left side. You should hear *3* distinct sounds: Heel-pull-back. Count: one and a (right), two and a (left) . . .

4 The right foot lands on the ball of the foot, slightly behind the left (Beat 3).

5 The right heel lowers making Beat 4, while the left heel simultaneously rises. Repeat with the other leg. You should hear *4* distinct sounds. Count: and and a one . . .

with Derek Hartley

Get a Bellyful of This

It came as quite a surprise to hear from Tina Hobin that Belly Dancing, her speciality, is one of the oldest known dance forms. Dating back to the first century BC, it was practised as far afield as Hawaii. Like many dance forms it was kept alive by the travelling gypsies of India and the exotic gyrations of the Spanish Flamenco owe more than a passing debt to a 'shimmering' gypsy dancer. It's fascinating how all these remarkable dance forms have survived the passage of time and taken on their subtle changes as they passed from one country to another.

Eventually taken up by the 'Ghawazee' of Egypt, travelling players who danced unveiled for the amusement of the crowds, the dance was performed by members of the hareem to celebrate such festivities as birth and marriage. Curiously enough as it became more commonplace for women not to expose themselves in public it was the young men, the 'Khawals' who, braiding their hair and applying kohl much as the women, took the belly-dance out onto the streets again. Indeed it is still performed by the men in local villages throughout the Middle East, much in the manner of Morris Dancing here in England.

The women, however, preferred to dance this solely for their own pleasure and entertainment and much as it caused shock and outrage when it first appeared at exhibitions throughout the Western World in the 1890s, it had become for them a very vital process for natural and healthy child-birth. I spoke to Tina about this and other aspects of belly-dancing, which I suppose for most of us seems quite unexpected, as so often we think of it as nothing more than an exotic display, guaranteed to win your man!

'Belly dancing is now being recognised as a health giving exercise, an art form even, which is also an exciting way to keep fit. A perfect opportunity to let your imagination take over and create your own fantasies! The dance steps themselves relax and stimulate, toning up the whole body, improving poor circulation, tightening weak and flabby muscles and loosening stiff joints. It is also an excellent way of relieving depression and tension.

'Of course there is no doubt that belly dancing is both sensual to watch and perform and its combination of undulating movements and graceful fluidity have led to its current increase in popularity as a sophisticated and disciplined form of exercise.'

A dancer herself for many years, Tina assured me that all was possible as I tried to master the 'shimmering' movement which was much like patting your head and rubbing your tummy at the same time. Apparently it all comes in time. Certainly the exotic perfume of burning joss sticks and the surrounding ladies in their colourful skirts and scarves gave all the authenticity and encouragement one was ever likely to want!

But belly-dancing and pregnancy? Tina went on to explain: 'Pupils claim that this form of dancing has enhanced their lives in many subtle ways, firming up their tummy muscles or improving a bustline. For many it has been an invaluable help after undergoing major surgery or childbirth and this is because the nature of the dance is so soothing. Many women have danced their way through pregnancy using the rotary movements and the pelvic tilts which gently massage the body and strengthen the lower spine, helping to relieve stress and pain.'

There may not be a suitable class near you but Tina has kindly given us one of her basic exercises which you might like to try, and if all else fails, well, you can always swathe yourself in the net curtains and amuse your friends for the evening!

BELLY DANCING

An exotic dance form of ancient origin, it has been performed in Temples and Hareem alike. First introduced to the West in 1893, it has gained considerable popularity as a sophisticated way to keep fit.

Benefits

The 'shimmering' hip movement and undulating tummy rolls are said to be condusive to healthier child-birth, and as an exercise form it is generally acknowledged to be excellent for muscle tone, as well as relieving tension and strain.

Further Reading

Tina Hobin: *Belly Dancing for Health and Relaxation* (Duckworth)
Wendy Buenaventura: *Belly Dancing* (Virago)

Try it yourself . . .

Starting position:
1 Hold your arms out to the side, bending the elbows slightly and turning the wrists up so that the palms of the hands are facing outwards.
2 Stand with your feet apart in line with your hips.
3 Elevate: i.e. lift your rib cage and push out.
4 Pull in your tummy, tightening the abdominal muscles.
5 Bend your knees slightly.

Hip rotation:
1 Push your right hip out to the right side.
2 Push the pelvis forward as far as you can, and then roll the hips over to the left.
3 Push the pelvis back to the rear, sticking your bottom out. Roll the hips over to the right (just a you would if using a hula hoop).
4 Continue working from (2) and (3).
5 Rotate the hips several times in a large smooth circle, then repeat rotating them in the opposite direction.

Hip shimmy:
1 Assume starting position.
2 Gently move the right hip forward, as you pull the right hip back, move the left hip forward.
3 Continue alternating the hips forward and backwards, starting slowly and working up to a fast tempo.

Pelvic Tilt:
1 Assume starting position.
2 Tighten your buttocks, thrust the pelvis forwards and tilt upward.
3 Relax the buttocks and push back.
4 Again, tighten your buttocks, thrust the pelvis forwards and tilt upward.
5 Relax buttocks, push the pelvis back. Repeat several times.

Raquel Welch and the
Hollywood interpretation. . .

The Wonders of the East

Yoga: the most peaceful of all exercises. And it is one of the rare forms of exercise that doesn't hurt you . . . or *shouldn't* anyway. Yet yoga is much more than just a fitness programme. When properly taught it provides as much spiritual as physical benefit, though that aspect is what sometimes puts people off. Still, it's up to you to choose whether or not you want to follow the spiritual theories, since they are by no means essential to the exercises which will help your body, even if you don't want to include your mind for the moment.

The great thing about yoga is that it is for any age and any shape because it's not about song and dance like many of the other kinds of exercise we see nowadays. The word *yoga* means union, and what yoga sets out to do is 'unite the body, the mind and the spirit in a harmonious balance with the universe.' It can exercise everything from your intestines to the hair on your head, but the five basic yoga principles are: proper exercise, breathing, relaxation, diet and positive thinking (meditation).

The movements have to be performed *slowly*, concentrating on gracefulness and rhythm, with a short motionless 'holding' stage in some positions. Nobody should ever try to strain their body into impossible positions: the rule is to go just as far as

you can, whatever that may be, and eventually the stretching movements will make your body supple enough to do the most unbelievable contortions.

Yoga is a Hindu discipline which is very old: in fact, the book containing the original yoga instructions was written in 300BC, though even that probably borrowed on some very ancient traditions. These 'Yoga Sutras' as they are called, stress that the natural goal of the technique is to free the mind from attachment to the senses so that the soul, once freed, can become united with the universal spirit. But most of us in the west are happy to borrow the yoga methods just to improve self-control, posture and health. The genuine 'yogi' probably sees that as a perversion of the discipline, but then clothes were once just something to keep us warm, weren't they?

YOGA

A series of postures and poses that affect almost every part of the body. Of antique origin it is associated with spiritual development and well-being and is not considered an exercise technique as such although the benefits are now generally well recognised.

Benefits

It is highly suitable for a wide variety of ages and body-types. Less likely to cause strain than a conventional exercise class, it is recommended for those people who are very unfit and would like to start getting into shape, but at their own pace. Yoga improves breathing and posture and is said to benefit the circulation and health of all the major internal organs.

Further Reading

B. K. S. Iyengor: *Light on Yoga* (Mandala)
Lynn Marshall: *Wake Up to Yoga* (Ward Lock)

'Salute to the Sun'

This particular version of the 'Salute to the Sun' is an ideal exercise to be done on rising or before going to bed. It strengthens and tones the entire body and coupled with correct breathing gives a sense of well-being. Do it slowly.

The action of the breath is very important – try to co-ordinate the movement of the body and the breath together.

1 Stand tall but relaxed – breathe naturally and empty your mind of thoughts.

2 Bring the hands together in front of the chest, with elbows out at right angles to the shoulders. *Breathe in*.

3 As you *breathe out* stretch the arms up and behind you, looking upwards, opening out the upper part of the chest. Breathe in.

4 As you *breathe out*, bend over and stretch out as far in front of you as you can, with heels and palms on the floor.

5 As you *breathe in* touch the knees, chest and forehead to the floor, arching the lower spine (elbows bent, hands beneath armpits).

6 As you *breathe out*, press through and upwards, curving the spine and stretching the front of the chest.

7 As you *breathe in*, curl the toes under and press the body back into a high right angle. There will be a strong 'pull' down the backs of the thighs. *Breathe out*.

8 As you *breathe in* bring one leg forward, with the knee bent into the chest, and *breathe out*.

9 *Breathe in* and join the extended leg to the front leg, keeping the head well tucked under and *breathe out*, and slowly stretch the backs of your knees.

10 Breathe in and breathe out as you slowly roll-up to the starting position. Repeat with a change of leg.

Aerobics Today Helps You Work, Rest and Play

Most of us imagine that aerobics arrived one day on a flight from Los Angeles somewhere at the bottom of Jane Fonda's handbag, but although we may have Jane to thank for its overnight success, the aerobics dance training was first devised fifteen years ago in America. Now it has become the most popular kind of exercise for women, with regular aerobics workouts on breakfast-time television. Kay Cornelius, who runs aerobics classes at Pineapple, explains why:

'It all started when a lady named Jackie Sorensen decided to adapt the standard exercise routines of the Canadian airforce by putting them to music and aiming them specifically at women. At the same time a similar programme was being developed by Dr Kenneth Cooper, who was working with patients who had had cardiac disease, and he put them on an aerobic recovery programme. This went against all the orthodox recovery programmes, which usually put the patients to bed and made them rest without getting up. With a very carefully supervised aerobic programme of walking and running, they recovered a lot faster, and they were much fitter and stronger than even before the disease, instead of becoming weaker as so many people do. Some of those patients even went on to run marathons! Within a few years classes were packed with equal numbers of men and women . . . even children, but the big commercial boom arrived when Jane Fonda began to publicise it.

To learn about aerobics I went over to America and worked in health clubs over there. When I came back there was nothing in this country – everybody was saying 'what's this *aerobatics* business?'! Nobody knew what it was. Now, suddenly, everybody wants to do it. But it's no miracle cure. It has taken you a long time to get unfit, so you are going to have to take time to get fit, taking it easy at first and building up. Anybody who has a medical problem should consult their doctor before starting aerobics. And be especially careful if you are *very* overweight or elderly.

'Aerobics means 'with oxygen', and the idea of the aerobics section of the class is to increase the body's demand for oxygen, because it's oxygen that gives you energy. You make the heart stronger and more efficient. You have more vitality. It also tones up your muscles, so you'll start to lose inches before you lose pounds, because the flab will turn to muscle and muscle weighs more than fat. I *look* as though I've lost a good stone or stone and a half in weight, but I actually weigh the same as when I started. The difference is that my clothes fit and everything looks tight, because the body contracts. Clench your legs now and you'll feel you have more room in your

The ordered dignity of the thirties contrasts sharply with the freer, more rigorous workouts of the eighties.

trousers. And eventually, of course, you can lose weight with aerobics.

'It has been shown medically that you should do some form of aerobic exercise three or four times a week. It can be jogging, swimming, squash . . . but it all depends on how it's done. Aerobics is about continuous, sustained exercise. Look at a businessman who goes to the squash court to try to work off his business lunches and his excess booze in the evenings. He may not be keeping fit at all: it depends on how he's playing his game. Rushing about the court in fits and starts, he is actually exercising *anaerobically*, which means without oxygen. To exercise aerobically you have to stay on the move all the time.

'An aerobic dance class is much more controlled than that. You don't have to be fit before you start, as long as you're sensible, because the whole point is that you can monitor your own programme within the class by taking your pulse. Yes, it *is* more strenuous than anything we have been used to in this country in terms of exercise classes. Until now all we've had here is the 'bend down touch your toes' kind of thing. But aerobics works! The first class may be a great shock to the system if you've never done

anything like it before, but that's the same with anything you do. In aerobics classes, just remember to be sensible. Don't try to keep up and compete. That's not what it's about. The responsibility is with you in the class.

'People often ask me how they can tell when they're working hard enough. Well, how *do* you know if you're overdoing it? Normally, you don't unless you get very red in the face and start to sweat. It is your heart beat that tells you various things, and by taking your own pulse rate you can monitor very carefully your own training programme. In my classes we take it *five times*, and from that people can judge if they've got to calm down or if they've got to put in more effort.

'It's because aerobics is so vigorous that it is now one of the fastest and healthiest ways of getting your body in shape. One last thing: anyone who may be too out-of-condition to start right away in a course of aerobics might be recommended to try a yoga or body-control class first. It doesn't take long to build up sufficient stamina to do almost any exercise or dance programme, but always bear in mind that pain is a *warning signal* that must not be ignored.'

AEROBICS

The word 'aerobic' defines any exercise that provides the body with oxygen and stimulates heart and lung activity. Several different routines come under the heading of aerobics and classes can include both dance and floor exercises.

Benefits

When properly taught, it increases cardiovascular (heart, lung) efficiency, tones the entire body and can be a specific help in maintaining weight loss when following a diet.

Further Reading

Kay Cornelius: *Kay Cornelius' Workout* – tapes and booklets available from Pineapple Mail Order

Looking After the Bodywork

John Gordon putting Dame Edna through her paces

It can be a mystifying experience entering a dance centre these days. In the early days when one was confronted with terms such as Ballet, Tap or Jazz, they were, even for a layman, fairly self-explanatory. Now, we're surrounded by Aerobics this, and Aerobics that, Calisthenics, Autogenics, California Stretch, Workouts, and a whole host of others too numerous to mention. As each teacher perfects and establishes their own personal style, so they search out a suitable title which they trust will give some indication of the type of class they teach. For the less informed however, sorting out 'Body Glow' from 'Shape Workout' can test the skills even of our highly informed reception staff. But for many, no term seems more perplexing than that of 'Body Conditioning', I think because it is so loosely applied and covers a broad spectrum of dance/exercise classes. A wide variety of such classes are taught at Pineapple, and it seems safe to say that they are extremely popular with all age groups and fitness levels. Perhaps for many of us they're the most approachable thing if our last memory of being fit conjures up visions of navy bloomers groaning away on the hockey pitch!

Sandy Strallen, who starred in Andrew Lloyd Webber's most recent success, 'Song and Dance', has prepared a version of his ever-popular class at Pineapple, which you can follow in detail at the back of the book. We also spoke to John Gordon and Sylvia Caplin, two of our most popular teachers and living proof, if any was needed, that 'looking after the bodywork' pays dividends.

With highly trained dance backgrounds, they have each formulated a slightly different technique, but one where the aim is essentially the same: to condition the body through exercises, without unnecessary strain or 'faddish' demands. Based largely on no-nonsense exercises, these routines might have as their influences the disciplines of yoga, or ballet, or indeed any number of permutations devised over the years, which give strength with suppleness to anyone from fifteen to seventy.

John Gordon, a teacher at Pineapple from the first day, encourages fitness and stamina, combined with strength and assurance. Cajoling and humouring in that gently wicked way of his, he gets you over those inhibitions that weigh you down throughout the day, meanwhile making the body fitter and healthier, more able to cope with the wear and tear. John, who shaped the body that turned Dame Edna Everage from ordinary housewife and superstar, into an overnight Megastar, obviously has the magic touch! His rapid 'Ten minute wake-up' is to be done in the shower and before breakfast, and it really works.

Sylvia Caplin also agreed to let a few secrets out when we asked how at a totally unmentionable age, she managed to eclipse just about anything in sight at Pineapple, and her brief exercises for hips and buttocks are also in this section for you to try.

I always send people to John, Sylvia and Sandy, with complete confidence, safe in the knowledge that they are backed by all those *essential* years of dance

Buster Bloodvessel of Bad Manners tries the workout!

BODY CONDITIONING

Various exercises designed to stretch and strengthen the body without requiring you to put steps together and dance. A combination of calisthenics, aerobics and other keep fit exercises with different programmes developed by each teacher.

Benefits

Ideal for many age groups and body types – it is a good stepping stone towards more organised dance techniques which require more particular skills. These classes offer plenty of variety while remaining relatively uncomplicated to master.

Further Reading

Bob Anderson: *Stretching* (Pelham Books)

training and experience, and they also possess a degree of caring for their respective students which is a hallmark of any teacher really worth their salt.

Body conditioning kept me sane through those early days of opening Pineapple, and no problem no matter how pressing kept me from that daily class.

For people like me who love the idea of dancing but somehow always end up having two left feet, I think Body Conditioning offers the best alternative. There's nothing like disappearing in a class, full of everyone from your daughter to your auntie, sweating away the cares of the day.

Sylvia's Slimmers and Shapers

Outer thigh slimmer
Sit on the buttocks – leaning backwards slightly, resting on the palms of your outstretched hands. Cross your ankles in front of you, placing your left foot in front. Raise your right thigh, then bring it down to the floor, and repeat this slapping action 8 times. Repeat with the other leg.

Inner thigh toner
Place yourself as illustrated with one leg extended to the side – with the foot flexed. Raise the leg waist high and lower again – repeat 8 times. Change legs and repeat.

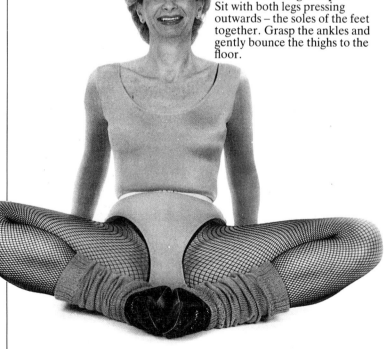

Buttocks and thigh shapers
Sit with both legs pressing outwards – the soles of the feet together. Grasp the ankles and gently bounce the thighs to the floor.

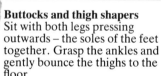

More buttocks and thigh shapers
Sit on the buttocks, with the arms slightly behind you to support your weight. Place the soles of the feet together and rock from side to side 16 times.

John's Ten Minute Wake-up

There's nothing too strenuous about these exercises – they only take a few minutes and really help you to start the day feeling relaxed and invigorated.

While you're in the shower . . .

Scalp Tugs (left and above)
Place fingers at the temples and push firmly into hair, making fists as close to the roots as possible. Tug forward firmly – moving the scalp, but keeping the head still – then tug backwards. Gradually increase the speed of movement and number of tugs. Then repeat the same movements in the back section of the head. This will help your hair look better, promote a healthier growth, and clear a muggy head.

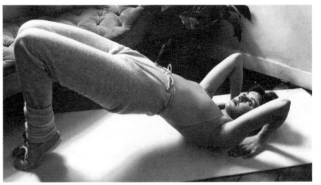

. . . and before you have breakfast

Back Push-up
This strengthens your back and thighs, and helps slim the waist. Lie flat on the floor, bend the knees, and draw your feet up close to your bottom. Place the hands beside the ears flat on the floor, elbows straight up. Inhale through the nostrils, and push the buttocks upwards, heels off the floor, shoulders on the floor. Hold for 4 counts. Exhale and lower the body to the floor. Repeat the exercise trying the advanced posture, raising first one leg and then the other.

Scalp Massage
Thinning and loss of hair are partly hereditary, but a tight scalp and bad circulation certainly don't help. A vigorous scalp massage while shampooing will improve scalp condition, and a temple and facial massage relaxes tension too.

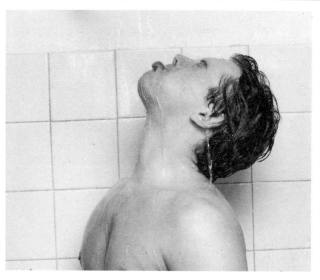

Jaw Lifts
A particularly good exercise for keeping away or improving a double chin. Look directly up at the ceiling, sticking your chin out as far as it will go. Now bring your jaw up towards your top lip, keeping your head well back. You should feel a huge stretch under your jaw if you are doing it correctly. Drop your head for a moment, swallow slowly, and repeat the exercise.

Bicycling (left)
Lie flat on your back and turn your palms towards the floor, bend your knees into your chest and roll up onto your shoulders. Placing hands behind the waist, slowly straighten up the body and legs, if possible to a verticle position, breathing steadily. Hold for 4 counts. This will improve your circulation. Then start to 'cycle'. Bring your legs together and go into:

The Plough (above)
Place the legs behind the head and toes on the floor. This helps alleviate tension in the shoulders and neck, and increases spine flexibility. Unwind back first, then legs, and end in a relaxed position lying on the floor.

Let's Get Physical and Mental

Only in the Body Control studio do you get the kind of one-to-one approach between teacher and pupil that ensures you are doing exactly the right exercise for your particular needs. The system is very specialised, but it is not physiotherapy. It is a technique in its own right, but it is also a stepping stone to other programmes. It is of particular benefit to dancers and people with back problems or other injuries, but it is just as useful to men and women who want to get fitter without building up extra muscle. So what exactly is Body Control?

What Michael King and his team teach is based on the Joseph Pilates Method, named after the man who developed it in New York around 1930. What he was trying to do was find a technique to help dancers who were injured, so that they could carry on exercising even with the injury. There was nothing specific around, so he borrowed things from yoga, ballet and other systems as the basis for a mat-work class. First he taught the mat-work class himself, and you can try many of these exercises yourself if you turn to page 110. Gradually he devised special machinery that he called the

Universal Body Reformer to refine the exercises still further. He was trying to avoid the idea of exercising through 'unnatural' movements, and worked on ones that were more 'natural'. And instead of building up bulky muscles, his intention was to lengthen them and stretch them more. Really, what you have to do is *learn one exercise properly rather than many badly.*

The machines help isolate sections of the body for special treatment: the plié machine, for instance, holds the trunk in place. You lie on your back and your body is held there naturally while you exercise the legs. Lying on the machine also encourages better posture and teaches you to stand up straight, helping to correct the all too familiar over-arched spine.

After isolating the legs, you might go on to isolate the stomach, keeping the body still, with the legs slightly supported in the air. Particular attention is paid in this technique to flexibility of the spine and strengthening the lower abdomen. Try using the stomach, for example, to get up from the chair – it's quite different from using your back. Or try this quick exercise of Michael's:

Stand with your back flat against the wall, but with your legs together and feet a little way out – about twelve inches – in front of you. Imagine your tummy button is pressed against your spine. Stay there for a few minutes and feel it. Now, just walk away, still trying to keep that feeling. Keep the back straight, try not to over-arch the spine. Did you feel the difference?

Ideally one should follow the specially devised programme for three sessions a week of an hour each, because after an hour the body gets tired and just leaves the strong muscles working while the weak ones give up and rest. The very first class is for your teacher to get to know what you want, and what your body needs. Gradually you get to know the routine, and you keep advancing your programme. One week you might be hanging upside down with steel clamps around your ankles, another you could be working with small weights. But you've got to learn to walk before you can run! Don't suddenly begin some over-strenuous exercise programme until you've learned about your own body, otherwise

Michael helping me to keep in shape

BODY CONTROL

Based on the Pilates Method, developed in the 1930s. Individual routines devised for use with specialist equipment. Primarily to strengthen and condition an injured or out-of-condition body.

Benefits

One to one teacher/student relationship. Safe, and ideal for absolute beginners. Tones the entire body, increasing strength and suppleness particularly of the stomach and back.

Further Reading

Philip Friedman and Gail Eisen: *The Pilates Method* (Warner Books)

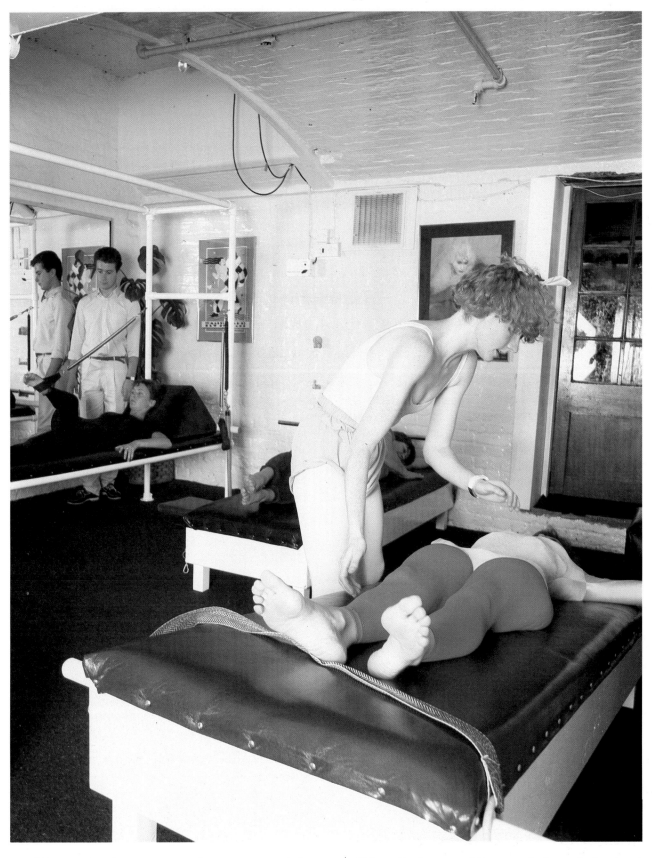

you'll just make the strong muscles stronger and the weak ones weaker. And according to Michael, instead of feeling happy after a workout, too many people feel absolutely worn out by the end of it. You don't have to kill yourself to feel good, but you must expect to ache a bit if you are totally out of

condition. Body control is no magic formula for weight control. If anything it simply changes fat into muscle and moves it around. You may even put on a little weight. But don't panic. According to Michael all you should do is stop getting on the scales and just start looking in the mirror!

47

Weights and Measures

Giles Webster runs the gymnasium at Pineapple West, which contains not only every imaginable shape and size of weights, but all the latest 'captive weight' equipment. He doesn't look a bit like Charles Atlas, so I asked him whether the gym was for bodybuilding, or could anyone have a go?

'Your muscles should be able to supply you with any movement you ask of them, within reason. If I ask you to do some press-ups, you will be able to. If I ask you to do a deep knee-bend with one leg, you can do it. In other words, what your body was designed to be able to do, it can now do . . . for a fairly protracted period of time. It's general exercise.'

Once a somewhat disreputable sport, weightlifting has long been a part of the physical fitness mainstream, becoming not only respectable, but now highly popular among women as well as men. The millions who now regularly 'pump iron' as part of their shaping-up programme, including athletes in many sports as well as dancers, derive several benefits. Not only does the body become stronger, it is also proportioned into a fresh symmetry . . . which does *not* mean you'll come out looking like an over-developed Tarzan, something Giles is especially aware that ladies may be afraid of. Because of a woman's hormone structure, she can increase strength with no increase in muscle bulk at all, and many of today's women body-builders, like Lisa Lyon, show how beauty can be enhanced by weight training. Women have much less muscle tissue than men, so the chances of building up big muscles are remote. But within each person's physiological limits, weight-training can have an astonishing effect.

First of all you try a little bit of most things around the gym (with Giles watching you, making sure you're not doing too much or hurting yourself), testing to see just how strong you are, whether you have any muscle problems, learning how the machinery works and what effect it's having on your body. And *you* tell him what *you* want: whether it's just to firm everything up or to fill the sleeves of a T-shirt . . . whatever. Giles is well aware that most of us if we admit it, are interested in looking better, and part of the training in the gym is specifically – though *not* exclusively– cosmetic.

When they've discovered your weak spots, they help you to work on them. For dancers, this can be crucial: professional dancers are very strong and fit for what they're doing, but often ballet training leaves the upper abdomen, thorax and upper- and lower-back relatively ignored, so weight-training is used to help the

Building bulk in the bad old days – definitely not recommended!

GYM'LL FIX IT

boys, for instance, achieve the co-ordination they require to do a lift, giving them enough physical strength with some reserve left for safety.

The only reason we've got muscles at all is to cope with gravity. If there were no gravity, we'd need only sparse musculature to help us move. So we use weight-training to give muscles more power to do more work than they're used to. And because muscles are brilliantly designed things, they rise to that challenge very well. Basically there are four variables that are combined to achieve those various effects:

1. The weights you use.
2. The distance you move them.
3. The number of times you move them.
4. The speed at which you move them.

By juggling with those, the exercises provide different results. You just have to tell your instructor what you would be happy with, and they'll tell you how long it will take to get there. *But* your idea of what you'll be happy with may change as you train! Giles guarantees that you will *feel* an effect within about ten workouts, and that you will *see* an effect somewhere between fifteen and twenty.

Naturally, if you drink a bottle of Scotch, smoke a hundred cigarettes or force-feed yourself with doughnuts in between visits, then, OK, he's going to have a hard time keeping up with you. But assuming you're treating the course responsibly and assuming you work according to what has been prescribed, then that is the guarantee. One fifty-nine-year-old lady who has never taken any exercise in the last forty-five years came in after her fifth class, and told everybody that the day before she had run up the stairs. What's so special about that? Well, the last time she had ever done it was when she was still *at*

school. Another lady just wanted to be able to squeeze her husband until it hurt! And the husband? Well, he complained to Giles. But that probably reflects more about the tender state of his machismo than anything else.

Once you have bought the right equipment, you can always do weight-training at home, though the problem, as Giles himself admits, is that it's *very boring*. And it's very hard work by yourself . . . that's why it's nice to come to a gym. There are people around who will encourage you. And most importantly, the captive-weight machine takes care if you make mistakes: if everything suddenly goes wrong, you can't drop it on your foot!

GYM

Exercises that use a system of weights and various types of machinery to increase the body's natural strength, and to shape and condition specific areas through isolation of muscle groups.

Benefits

Usually there are only a small number of people exercising at any one time, allowing a close teacher/student relationship. Hard work shows definite results after six to eight weeks.

Further Reading

Charles Gaines: *Staying Hard* (Papermac)

Weight training doesn't necessarily mean you have to end up looking like Charles Atlas, as Lisa Lyon (right) quite clearly demonstrates

Child's Play

You can't move on a Saturday for children at Pineapple! They are there quite literally in their hundreds! Imaginative dance, Ballet, Tap and Fame, the list goes on; and such has been the demand that we've even started a little company for them to provide some sort of a goal and lend encouragement. Not that they really need it.

I do think the sight of all those eager young faces is immensely pleasing to see. With all the marvellous children's wear we have designed for the shop, it looks like someone has tipped dolly mixtures all over the studio floor! But training children, as I'm sure all parents know, is an art in itself and we are lucky enough to have the right people teaching this essential area for us.

One aspect that I was keen to do away with at Pineapple was the idea of having to do anything for a whole 'term', which invariably means sobbing children and worn out mothers getting to a class that neither dare miss. At Pineapple you should be able to find your class, as you left it, much like the professional dancers that use our facilities. In other words, if you want to come in for your class then it's there and if not, well mummy isn't going to age overnight and you're still going to be a ballerina or a John Travolta when you grow up, if that's what life has in store for you. I think it's absolutely essential that children enjoy dancing for its own sake and I really can't stress this enough. Dancing has to be one of the most natural things that any of us first attempt to do and it does seem both unnecessary and a shame to cloud this enthusiasm with 'technique' and too strict a discipline. I think 10 or even 11 is a suitable age to start teaching a child serious technique if he or she shows signs of a promising career in ballet, and perhaps a little (in some cases a lot) older for the other techniques. Don't forget that we are dealing

with young developing bodies that are changing all the time, so great care must be taken in finding a good, well-qualified teacher for everyone's peace of mind.

It almost seems unnecessary to say it in these liberated times, but the stigma about young boys in dance classes still seems to cling. If I could just get everyone into Pineapple for a day and you could see for yourselves the eagerness and imagination they possess, I feel confident I could change that thinking in a flash. As for the male dancers that come to us, I hope they continue to show by example the extraordinary discipline and devotion that is required by any dancer to survive in what is a largely unglamorous career.

So if you have any children's dance classes near you and your young son wishes to attend, give him the encouragement he needs; we still remain one of the few countries where for some bizarre reason it is considered effeminate rather than virile to be seen as a male dancer!

We haven't included a section for children at the back of this book because we feel it warrants a book all of its own, and we hope it won't be too long before that's forthcoming. Meanwhile if you can't keep this out of the clutches of your twelve-year-old who wants to be the next Bonnie Langford, let her try some things for herself or himself, but keep an eye on them. Famous last words; last time she was home on holiday, my energetic nine-year-old took herself off on a horrifying schedule of about five classes in one day, including two aerobic classes. Talk about making us feel our age! I have to confess that this kind of routine is not recommended, either for adults or for children.

Fashion Gets Physical

The mood of the eighties is decidedly one of leisure combined with health and fitness, and where else would that mood be more instantly reflected than in the clothes we wear? Loose-fitting trainers and track-suits, sharp colours, jogging shoes – all worn outside the gym and in the street have brought about a minor revolution in the way we look. Diana Ross and Olivia Newton John both told us to 'work that body' and 'get physical', and the world's fashion designers have been urging us to 'look physical'. Not only has exercise taken pride of place over drinking and dining as a sparetime activity, it has also become the leading contender for topics of conversation, way ahead of firm favourites like sex and the weather. The imagery is clearly in line with our gleamingly fit bodies: clothes that were originally worn only by athletes and dancers have already become essentials in everybody's wardrobe. The look is relaxed and utilitarian, the feel is loose and warm . . . the grey, fleecy lined sweatshirt has been adapted into almost every style and appeared with almost every designer's distinguishing symbol.

As our lives have become more and more geared towards leisure, we have needed the leisure wear to go with it. Most people don't like the constraints of a conventional suit or that formality of twin-set and pearls. When Jane Fonda appeared in her aerobics book wearing a striped leotard, everybody in aerobics classes wanted a striped leotard. As soon as the Kids from Fame appeared wearing leg warmers, the kids of the world took to leg warmers as easily as their parents had switched from pressed trousers to blue denim. The leg warmer that once had (and still does) a practical use in the dance studio, has now become a fashion accessory.

And these days, the trend is often for teenagers to identify with dance groups like Fame and Hot Gossip, as opposed to pop groups, whose image is often bizarre, extreme and inaccessible. Once there was Beatlemania, now there's dancemania. And designers like Norma Kamali in the States and Jeff Banks in Britain have seen the possibilities for turning it into a look that has been instantly and internationally adopted as today's favourite street fashion.

Because we at Pineapple feel we are so experienced in all aspects of dance, we decided that we would have the best ingredients for designing and marketing our own range of dancewear and leisure wear, and our operation now manufactures clothing for worldwide distribution.

Dancewear is fun for everyone . . . shown here by my daughter Lara (right) and Arlene Phillips' daughter, Alana

Dressing up (and down) for dance: the girl on the left is wearing a suitable selection of clothes to keep the muscles warm and flexible – one that allows for maximum comfort and freedom once the body is thoroughly warmed up. Don't forget to keep warm after class as well!

Bonnie Langford and friends wearing just some of the extraordinary range of dance wear available today. . . .

56

Knitted in 2/12 yarn. 25 per cent wool, 75 per cent acrylic. Any 4 ply yarn can be used – either in a wool/acrylic or 100 per cent acrylic yarn, i.e. Tasmin, Torpedo etc., though for best results the yarn used in the pattern is recommended. This yarn is available from 'Rupertknits' at Pineapple, in twenty different colours.

Sizes

1. Small/medium (34″–38″)
2. Large (38″–40″) [Large size given in brackets throughout pattern]

Materials

200 grams of yarn in main colour; 1 gram of yarn in contrast colour for logo; 1 pair each of needle numbers 2¾mm and 4mm.

Tension

A recommended tension of 22 stitches and 30 rows to 10 cms, worked over stocking stitch. However this will vary according to the yarn used – so larger or smaller needles may be used where necessary.

Stitches used

1. K.2.P.2 Rib
2. Stocking stitch, i.e. 1 row knit, 1 row purl

Abbreviations

M.C. – main colour; C.C. – contrast colour; K. – knit; P. – purl; st. – stitch; st.st. – stocking stitch.

Instructions

With No. 2¾mm needles and M.C. cast on 112 [122] st.
Work 40 rows in K.2.P.2. Rib.

Next Row: Change to No. 4mm needles and increase 10 st. thus:
K.11 * Knit into front and back of next st., K.9 [10] **.
Repeat from * to ** 10 times. K. to end. 122 [132] st.

Next row: purl to end.
Continue in st.st. for 73 [83] more rows.

75th [85th] row: working from diagram place stitches for first row of pattern as follows:
Knit 37 [42] st. Join in C.C. where indicated by the pattern (pattern to be worked right to left on K. rows, left to right on P. rows). Care should be taken not to pull threads too tight at back of work.

Continue in pattern until row 24 is completed. Cast on 10 st. at beginning of next and following row: 142 [152] st., while continuing with pattern to Row 47.

Continue until 54 [62] rows have been worked for sleeve (in total, from cast on).

Next row: with right side facing, K.40. Cast off 62 st., continue to end (note: cast off must be loose).

Next row: K.40. Turn and cast on 62 st., turn and continue with 40 st., to end.

Work second half of sleeve to match front. Cast off 10 st., at beginning of next and following rows: 122 [132] st.

Work back to match front.

With right side facing, decrease 10st. on next row thus:
K.11 *K.2 together, K.9 [10]**. Repeat from * to ** 10 times.
K. to end: 112 [122] st. remain. Change to No. 2¾mm needles and work 40 rows in K.2.P.2. Rib. Cast off loosely in Rib.

Collar: with right side facing, pick up and knit 62 st., along back of neck. Work 5 rows in K.2.P.2. Rib. Cast off loosely in rib. Work front of neck to match back.

To make up

Join side and sleeve seams.
Sew sides of neck rib.
Contrast threads on wrong side of work should be woven into the back.
Sew in loose ends.
Do not press.

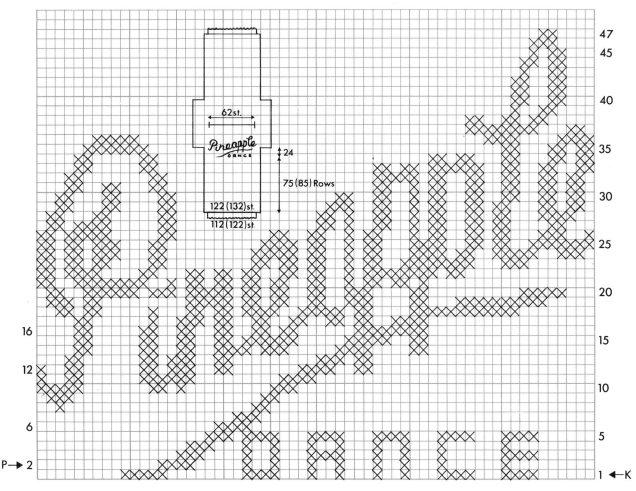

Part 2
THE FITNESS FACTS

Since the very beginnings of Pineapple, I've always believed that dance should be fun, but since lots of people are using it as a way to keep fit, I feel it's terribly important to be aware of the medical aspects of exercise. It's a controversial subject, I know, but we are lucky enough to have the benefit of advice from leading medical experts in different fields, on which this section is based.

There is no doubt that the dance boom which began in this country in the mid-Seventies has been inextricably linked with a growing interest in health. In the last few years, we have begun to think of health not merely as the absence of illness, but as a positive state of well-being – physically, mentally and emotionally – in other words, fitness.

When you're fit, day-to-day living is easier. You can cope better with crises, you can put more into life and therefore get more out of it, and since you feel good and look good, your morale is high. We have also begun to see fitness as something for which we can take responsibility ourselves rather than simply leaving it to doctors. It's ironic that while medical science has made astonishing progress in many areas, it has also become clear that most of the modern killer diseases – coronary heart disease, for example, lung disease and some forms of cancer – are to a large extent self-inflicted, and that by taking better care of ourselves we can in many cases prevent them.

Fitness is the result of several factors – eating sensibly, getting enough sleep, not smoking or drinking to excess, and of course getting enough exercise.

The human body was designed to thrive on tough physical effort – hunting for food, escaping from preditors, walking great distances, moving heavy weights. It was certainly not designed for sitting at desks all day, and being transported from place to place in cars, lifts, or heaven help us, moving walkways! Modern living has taken all the exercise out of our daily lives, and so in order to get fit, we have to build it back in again. And most of the medical experts are agreed that dance is the ideal way of doing it because it contains all the elements that good exercise should have. For a start, dance uses every single part of your body and it contains a large element of 'aerobics', which is certainly one of the buzz words of the eighties. What it means, literally, is 'with oxygen', and it describes the kind of continuous exercise, like jogging, cycling and swimming that gets your heart and lungs working harder over a period of time, making them stronger and more efficient. Dance also works on individual muscles, strengthening them and improving their tone so that they become firmer and your body becomes more shapely. It improves your posture and helps you move much more easily and gracefully. It is also non-competitive, allowing you to work on your own body at your own pace, a point worth remembering when you join a class and find yourself next to someone who can do it all perfectly without so much as a single bead of sweat appearing on her unwrinkled brow! Moving to music is also very satisfying emotionally, allowing you to express yourself in a physical way, and last, but by no means least, dance is tremendous fun! There is no point in coming up with the most efficient exercise

programme in the world if it's so boring that nobody wants to do it more than once. The joy of dance is that there is an almost infinite variety of styles on offer, so that if you reach the point where you feel you've had enough of one, there are plenty of others to keep you going for a lifetime!

How Fit Are You?

Before you embark on any programme of exercise, it's a very good idea to know just how fit you are, not only to prevent you from coming to any harm, but to help you choose a programme which will suit your individual needs, and to give you a goal to aim at. If you don't know how fit you were when you started, you have no way of gauging with any accuracy how well you are progressing, and it could be that the particular exercise routine you have chosen is not helping you at all in the areas where you most need help. If you're completely honest with yourself, you'll have a reasonably good idea whether or not you are fit. If you have done no exercise at all since you left school, and find yourself gasping for breath and unable to speak for a few minutes after you've run ten yards for a bus, then you know you are pretty unfit!

If you have ever suffered from high blood pressure, any heart disorder (or have had rheumatic fever), arthritis, lung problems, or you are more than two stone overweight, you should consult your doctor before you start any programme of exercise. Most NHS doctors will be only too happy to check you over, but some may feel that it's over and above the normal call of duty, like a medical for a life insurance policy, and will charge a small fee.

If you feel you are reasonably fit and have no medical problems, then you might find there are facilities at the place where you attend classes for

carrying out a few, very basic, but helpful, fitness assessment tests, like the Harvard Step Test.

All the equipment you need is a step 18 inches high (20 inches for men), a metronome (either an electronic one, or the old fashioned, piano-lesson type), and a watch with a second hand. If you want to do it at home though, you can substitute the second step of the staircase, and ask someone to pace you with two steps each second. Of course the result will not be quite so accurate, but nevertheless it will provide a good general guide to your fitness level.

What you do is step up with your right foot, then with your left, down with your right foot, and then your left, repeating the whole sequence of movements 30 times in a minute (set the metronome to 120 beats a minute, which will give you the pace at which to work). Keep going for as long as you can, up to a maximum of five minutes. When you have finished the test, rest for one minute, and then take your pulse for 30 seconds. The formula for working out your Fitness Factor is:

$$\frac{\text{Seconds of work done} \times 100}{\text{Pulse count for 30 seconds} \times 5.5}$$

So, if you managed to keep going for the full five minutes (300 seconds) and your pulse rate over the 30 seconds was 70, your Fitness Factor is 80 (300 × 100 ÷ 70 × 5.5). As you exercise and get fitter, your pulse rate should drop, so if, a few months later, your pulse rate over the 30 seconds is down to 55, your Fitness Factor will be 100, which is pretty good. Always try and do the test under the same circumstances – in the same air temperature and at the same time of day – because outside factors could distort the result you get.

Taking your pulse after a few minutes of hard aerobic exercise will also give you some idea of the level at which you should be training. The maximum rate at which a heart can beat is 220 beats a minute,

diminishing by roughly one beat for every year of your life. When you start exercising, you should aim to get your heart beating at about 60 per cent of its maximum rate, *gradually* building up over a period of months to about 80 per cent, which is the ideal aerobic training rate. The chart on page 78 shows you how to calculate your own training rate.

To find out what your training rate should be, stop after you've been exercising hard for a few minutes, and take your pulse by pressing the fingers of your left hand onto the inside of your right wrist just below the base of your thumb (always assuming you don't wear your watch on your right wrist), and counting the beats for six seconds. Multiply that figure by ten to give you the rate for one minute. Incidentally, you should take your pulse the instant you stop exercising because 30 seconds after you stop, your pulse rate will be half way back to normal, and since this method does not allow for that fact, while the Harvard Step Test does, you might be misled into thinking that you're not exercising hard enough and push yourself more than you should.

While taking your pulse will tell you how hard your heart is working, it will not give you a total picture of your state of fitness by any means. According to Malcom Emery, head of Sports Sciences at the West London Institute who is closely involved in the *Sunday Times* 'Getting in Shape' programme, if you think of the body simply as consisting of heart, lungs, blood and muscle, then for someone who has not exercised for years, it's their muscles that will have deteriorated most. Heart and lungs deteriorate slowest of all, so even if you seem pretty fit according to a pulse count, your muscles could be in a terrible state, so that if you start exercising vigorously straightaway, you're running the risk of pulling, straining or even tearing something.

Both Malcom Emery and British Olympic team physiotherapist Vivian Grisogono agree that it makes sense to think about 'getting fit for getting fit' And if you think about it, after five, ten or even fifteen years of total inactivity, it is asking for trouble to throw yourself into a demanding programme of exercise with no preparation.

The key words in any exercise programme are *gently* and *gradually*. Muscles, for instance, should be stretched gently. One very common exercise is touching your toes, with the object of stretching your hamstrings – the group of muscles at the back of your thigh. But, if you haven't exercised for years, it will be impossible to touch your toes without a great deal of pain and possibly damage too. Even if you can only comfortably reach as far as your knees when you bend over, you are still stretching your hamstrings, but gently, and after a few weeks of doing that, you will be able to reach down to mid-shin and a few weeks later, you may well be able to touch your toes.

The ultimate goal

Malcolm Emery believes that if you've done no exercise for years, it will take about twelve weeks to get fit for getting fit. In the same way as there is no such thing as a successful 'crash' diet there is no such thing as a successful 'crash' exercise programme either. After all, it's taken years of neglect for your body to get out of shape, so it's unreasonable to expect it to become strong and supple in a couple of weeks.

A word about pain. Many people have got into a rather puritanical, not to say masochistic frame of mind about exercise, believing that unless it's hurting, it's not doing you any good. *All* the experts – doctors, physiotherapists, sports physiologists – agree that it simply is not true. It does *not* have to hurt to do you good – in fact, pain is nature's way of telling you to stop! If you feel pain in a muscle while you're working it – as opposed to a stretching sensation – you should not carry on. It is the same with cramp. What the muscle is telling you is that it's tightening up because you have worked it into a fatigued state. If you go on working it, it will tighten still further and possibly tear.

The 'burn' is another buzz word in exercise today – describing the burning sensation you get in a muscle when you've been working it hard. What has

happened is that you have pushed the muscle into an 'anaerobic' condition, which means you are making it work without oxygen, one of the fuels muscles need to work efficiently, which makes it very heavy going indeed. Vivian Grisogono believes that 'going for the burn' is asking for trouble because it can lead to the breakdown of the muscle, and she points out there is no scientific evidence whatsoever that it achieves any more than working the muscle *progressively* harder without feeling any pain.

You do hear top athletes talking about the 'pain barrier', or marathon runners referring to 'hitting the wall'. But it's not a *pain* barrier so much as a psychological barrier when they reach the point where their body is telling them that it has had enough and does not want to go on. If top athletes feel pain in a muscle, they stop immediately because they know that if they carry on using it, they run the risk of a serious injury which could put them out of action for months.

Obviously when you start working muscles that haven't been used for years, they are going to feel sore and stiff the following day, but they shouldn't be so stiff and painful that you can barely get out of bed or hobble down the stairs for the next few days. If they are, then you know you've overdone it, and should give it a rest for a few days. Don't try to 'work it out' by carrying on with the same exercise routine because you'll only make things worse, but there's no reason why you should not go swimming instead. When you do start again, take it gently, and don't overstrain your heart and lungs either. If you're exercising properly, you should be breathing hard at the end of the class, but not gasping for breath, unable to hold a normal conversation, or feeling sick. Pushing yourself too hard is counter-productive. If getting fit makes you feel awful, then you're simply not going to keep it up. And ideally, like a diamond, exercise is for ever!

Heart disease, often the consequence of the wrong diet, too much stress and not enough exercise, is a major killer today. In the past, it has killed far more men than women, but as increasing numbers of women find themselves in stressful careers, and subject to the unhealthy lifestyle that goes with them, the gap is beginning to narrow.

What your heart does, at its most basic, is pump blood round your body, carrying oxygen and other essential nutrients to all your organs – liver, kidneys, brain and so on – and to your muscles and other tissues, and carries away waste products, some of which are then filtered out by your kidneys, or in the case of carbon dioxide, by your lungs, in exchange for fresh oxygen. The heart is made largely from muscle, and if you exercise it – in other words, make it work harder than usual – it will become bigger and stronger, which means that it will be able to do the same amount of work with less effort.

No one knows for certain exactly what triggers your heart and lungs to start working faster when you exercise. Part of the reason, though, is that exercise makes the small blood vessels in your muscles and lungs open up so that the blood flows through them faster, your blood pressure drops and your heart responds to that drop by pumping faster. The fact that your muscles are working harder means that they are using more oxygen, and producing more carbon dioxide in the process which triggers your lungs to work harder, exchanging it for fresh oxygen.

As you get fitter and your heart and lungs get stronger, they can cope with the additional work with less effort, and that is why your pulse rate drops. As with any machinery, the more efficiently it works, and the less strain it's under, the longer it will last.

Exercise can help prevent heart disease in another way, too. One common cause of heart attacks is the narrowing or clogging up of the arteries, caused by too much cholesterol in the blood. The right amount of cholesterol is essential for repairing damaged tissues among other things, but in excess, it is

potentially dangerous, and while it makes sense to cut down the amount of cholesterol-rich food you eat (eggs, butter, cream and so on), it is worth remembering that only about 20 per cent comes from what you eat, while 80 per cent is manufactured in your liver. When you exercise regularly, you not only keep your arteries open which means they're less likely to narrow, but you also burn off the cholesterol which could clog them.

Since your muscles need a good supply of oxygen to burn up the fuel they need to work efficiently, it is obviously vitally important to breathe properly when you're exercising. Of course, breathing is something we all do all the time without giving it a second thought, but you may not be doing it as efficiently as you should. Always try and fill your lungs when you breathe in, and don't pant shallowly, only filling the top part of your lungs, though when you start exercising, one of the hardest things is remembering to breathe at all! When you're doing something strenuous, your instinct may well be to take a deep breath and hold it, which makes everything much more difficult.

Although you need a plentiful supply of oxygen when you're exercising, it is possible to have too much of a good thing, so don't be tempted to gulp in great lungfuls of air. If your muscles aren't burning up the oxygen you're taking in, then it will saturate your blood and temporarily swamp the centres in your brain which control your breathing, which will make you feel very dizzy, or even lose consciousness. It's very unlikely to happen while you are actually exercising because you'll be using up all the oxygen you're taking in, but it could happen when you stop.

Exercise and Your Muscles

We tend to think of muscles as those great, lumpy things all over Arnold Schwartzenegger, but in fact they are what enable you to stand upright, and move around. In that sense, you are using some of them all the time, but if you don't work them hard enough – or don't use some of them at all – they become weak so that everything you do, even if it's only sitting at a desk all day, becomes more tiring. Your muscles also lose tone, becoming flaccid and flabby, and covered with fat, and if you don't stretch them, they shorten as you grow older causing your whole frame to shrink. That's why you only ever hear people talking about '*little* old ladies'!

The object of exercising your muscles, then, is to make them stronger, more flexible, and to improve their tone, which will give them and you a better, firmer shape.

Flexibility comes from stretching exercises, and Vivian Grisogono believes that 'passive' stretching is the safest way to start because it is self-limiting – you can only stretch the muscles as far as they can go and no further. To stretch your hamstrings, for example, sit on the floor with your legs straight out in front of you, your hands on your thighs and your back straight. Then bend forward, sliding your hands down your legs as far as you can comfortably go. Hold that position for ten seconds, to allow the muscles to pay out to their fullest extent, then sit up again. If you do that every day, you will soon find your muscles becoming more flexible.

Vivian Grisogono believes that your calf muscles, particularly, will benefit from daily stretching, since they are the group most vulnerable to injury in women, not just because they are the group of muscles that works hardest in explosive, propulsive movements like jumping or sprinting, but because the hormonal changes that occur during the menstrual cycle increase the risk of spasm, while wearing high-heeled shoes shortens the muscles and makes them more likely to tear.

To stretch them safely, step forward with one leg, so that your feet are about 15–18 inches apart, bending that knee, and try to keep the back leg straight and the heel on the floor. If you can do it easily, then move your front foot a little further forward. As you hold that position, you should feel a stretching sensation in the calf muscles of your back leg. Reverse the process for the other leg. You can improve the strength and tone of your muscles by working them harder than usual in a number of different ways.

In Isometric exercises, you work the muscles by tensing and relaxing them without any movement. If you press the palms of your hands together and push hard, you feel the muscles in your arms tensing but you aren't actually moving them. It's not a particularly useful form of exercise for most people, though, because it only increases the strength and bulk of the particular muscles you're working on, and has no aerobic effect whatsoever. In fact, since it cuts off the supply of blood to the muscles while you're actually working them, it makes your heart strain to overcome the increased resistance, which could be dangerous if you suffer from high blood pressure.

In Isotonic exercise, the aim is to strengthen muscles and make them more flexible by using them to produce movement in two ways – *concentrically*, which means they are shortening to pull a limb up against gravity, and *eccentrically* which means stretching them out again to lower the limb in a controlled way when otherwise gravity would mean it simply flopped down again. If your arm is by your side, and you raise it to shoulder level, then your shoulder muscles are working concentrically. When you slowly lower it again, the same muscles are working eccentrically.

You can use weights in isotonic exercise to strengthen your muscles by making them work harder than normal, or, as in dance-based exercise programmes, you can use the weight of the limb itself, and reptition. Lying on your side on the floor,

and lifting your top leg up and down twenty times will certainly get the muscles in your thighs and bottom working hard!

You might be afraid of working your muscles too hard in case you wind up looking like a Russian Olympic shot-putter, but have no fear. All you will do is increase your muscle power, improve your muscle tone, and get rid of the fat covering your muscles, without increasing their bulk. Women have less muscle fibre than men, and even if you follow the same programme of exercise that will give a man huge biceps and triceps, it simply cannot have the same effect on you.

Exercise and Weight Control

Muscle is also a very important factor in controlling your weight through exercise. There are two types of muscle fibres – 'white' or 'fast twitch', and 'red' or 'slow twitch'.

'White' muscle is used for rapid, explosive movement, like sprinting, and works anaerobically – without oxygen, which is why you can only sustain this sort of exercise for a very short period of time. The fuel 'white' muscle uses is glycogen, a form of glucose manufactured from fat by your liver, about nine pounds of which is stored, in the proportions one part glycogen to three parts water, in your muscles and liver. When those stores are full, any excess fuel is stored as fat under your skin.

When you exercise anaerobically, your muscles use up glycogen so that your body's stores are depleted, and you may appear to have lost weight, but it is only temporary because what you've lost is glycogen and water, and your body will automatically replenish its stores next time you eat. What it does mean, of course, is that fat which otherwise would have been stored in that form under your skin is converted and stored as glycogen instead, so while exercising anaerobically – using 'white' muscle – doesn't actually take weight off, it can prevent you from putting any more on.

'Red' muscle, on the other hand, is used for sustained movement which requires stamina – long distance running, and any form of aerobic exercise. Initially when you start exercising aerobically, your muscles will burn up glycogen, but as you carry on, your liver can't convert fat into glucose and then into glycogen fast enough, and so the muscles start burning up fat directly. Unlike glycogen, your body will not automatically replace this fat afterwards, and so the weight you lose stays lost!

Whether you have more of one type of muscle fibre than the other seems to be largely the luck of the genetic draw, and though it is not clear whether you can increase the amount of 'red' muscle by exercising, it is known that if you don't exercise, 'red' muscle will degenerate into 'white'.

The speed at which your body converts food into fuel and burns it up is increased greatly while you're exercising because muscle is more active metabolically than fat. Since it takes some time to slow down again after you stop, by exercising aerobically for at least twenty minutes three or four times a week, you can get your body to carry on burning up fat at the faster rate all the time.

You might think that doing a lot of exercise will increase your appetite so much that you'll eat even more than your new, faster metabolic rate can burn up. But for most people, it doesn't seem to work out that way, and you may well find that after a class you want to eat less, not more.

Don't expect miracles, though. In fact, you may well find that for the first few months, your weight stays exactly the same, or even creeps up a little. But don't panic – there are several very good reasons why that might happen. For one thing, as you've been burning off fat, you have also been developing muscle, and muscle is heavier than fat. A better guide at this stage is inches rather than pounds. Although muscle weighs more, it takes up less space, so you may well find that the jeans you could only get on with a shoe-horn a few months ago are now so comfortable that you can eat in them, bend over without risking serious injury, and even breathe!

The other point worth remembering is that nature discriminates against women when it comes to body fat. The body of a lean, fit man will only have about 8 per cent fat, while the body of a lean, fit woman will have nearer 15 per cent, so that while you can work on your thighs, say, or your stomach, to improve the muscle tone and decrease the fat cover, you can't get rid of all the excess fat by exercise alone.

The answer is a combination of exercise and dieting, and 'dieting' *does not* mean a few weeks of eating nothing but paw-paw and baked beans, or grapefruit and hard-boiled eggs, and then reverting to your old habits – but a lifetime of healthy, sensible, balanced eating. After all, you're going to put a lot of effort into getting your body into good shape, so it's pointless to feed it on junk. In the last few years, dieting has become big business, with shelves full of diet aids, and hardly a week goes by without a diet book featuring on the bestsellers' list. But out of the welter of faddy dietary nonsense we have been exposed to in recent years, has emerged the view held by most nutritionists that the healthiest possible diet is one that is low in fat and sugar, and high in fibre; and equally important, it's one that most of us can fit into our daily lives without too much difficulty.

Until you start cutting down on the amount of fat you eat, you probably won't have realised just how much there is in your diet. It is not only in obvious things, like dairy products and fried food, but in pastry, cakes and biscuits, roasted nuts and crisps, and even avocado pears. To reduce your fat intake, try grilling food instead of frying it, or if you must fry, use a non-stick pan that needs no fat to lubricate it, and make sure you drain off any fat the food itself produces. If a recipe calls for sour or single cream, use low-fat yogurt instead, and used skimmed milk in tea, coffee, or on cereals. Many supermarkets and some milkmen stock it now, but if you can't find it, use the dried kind, or simply pour away the 'top of the milk' before you use it.

According to current dietary thinking, most of us eat far too much meat and don't need all the protein it gives us. Meat once or twice a week (once a month is quite sufficient for me), with fish, eggs, cheese, pulses (beans, lentils and so on) the rest of the time will provide all the protein your body needs.

As a nation, we also eat far too much sugar, white and brown, which explains why we are at the top of the world's tooth decay league and why about a quarter of us are overweight. Sugar is a simple carbohydrate which is converted instantly into glucose by the body and provides a rapid jolt of energy. But the sudden rise of sugar in the blood causes the liver to produce insulin to counteract it so that the sugar level drops sharply and the body craves more sugar.

Apart from providing instant energy, sugar does nothing else for your body at all, and any that isn't burned up is stored as fat. Your body can get all the sugar it needs from other complex carbohydrate foods – vegetables, fruit, whole grains (wholemeal bread for instance) and some pulses, so you can safely cut out all processed sugar from your diet.

The problem is that many people have a sweet tooth. If you are among them, and you can cut out all cakes or sweets from your diet, the thought of a bar of chocolate, or a piece of fudge cake becomes so irresistible that eventually, you succumb. You then feel so guilty that you have another piece to comfort yourself, and wind up abandoning your healthy eating habits altogether. If you want a piece of chocolate gâteau occasionally, then have it. It's strange the way human nature works, and you may find that now it is no longer Forbidden Fruit, you don't really want it after all.

Recently, salt has come under careful medical scrutiny, first in America (where many people have cut down the amount of salt they eat, or cut it out of their diet altogether) and more recently here. Certainly most of us eat more salt than our body

needs, and salt not only encourages your body to retain fluid, but there is strong evidence that it is an important factor in high blood pressure. It's unrealistic to try and cut salt out of your diet altogether, all in one go, but you can re-educate your palate to want less over a period of three or four weeks. Avoid salty foods like peanuts and crisps, cut down the amount of salt you use in cooking, and try not to add any at the table. If you reduce by half the amount of salt you use, you will be pleasantly surprised at how different many foods taste, because before the dominant taste was always salt.

As for vitamins, expert opinion varies. Some doctors believe that if you are eating a well-balanced diet, you're getting all the vitamins you need, and therefore you're simply wasting time and money by swallowing handfuls of vitamin tablets every day. Other doctors feel that so much of our food is processed and treated with chemicals which destroy the natural vitamins that you do need to supplement your intake with tablets. What is undeniably true is there is not the slightest point in living on junk food, swallowing handfuls of vitamin tablets, and then kidding yourself that you're giving your body everything it needs. According to recent research in America, an unrelieved diet of junk food is responsible for the reappearance of deficiency diseases, like beriberi, in young people, and there is also growing concern in America and Europe about the effect of the chemical additives (flavouring, colourings and preservatives) in processed food on our physical and mental health. All very good reasons, if any more were needed, for eating 'natural' foods and plenty of fresh fruit and vegetables.

When you eat is also an important factor in controlling your weight. Ideally, you should only eat when you are hungry, not just because it is lunchtime, although obviously you can control that to some extent by when you eat. If you have your main meal late at night, you probably will not feel hungry in the morning. It's not a good idea to eat a large meal late in the evening because your body will

not have enough time to metabolize the food properly before your whole system starts slowing down ready for sleep.

Ideally, you should always eat breakfast because it will give you the energy to get through the morning without flagging, and will stop you wanting a packet of biscuits or a danish pastry with your mid-morning coffee. Obviously it doesn't have to be the full British Railways number – cereal, eggs, bacon sausage, tomato, mushrooms, fried potatoes, toast and marmalade – a piece of wholewheat toast and an apple would do. But if you don't even have time for that, try blending a glass of orange juice, an egg, a dessertspoon of plain yogurt, and a teaspoon of honey if you have a sweet tooth. It is very nutritious, filling, tastes good and takes less than a minute to make the drink.

It is not a good idea to skip lunch because you will find yourself flagging later in the afternoon if you do, and if you're going to exercise that evening, you must provide the fuel your body will need if it's going to work hard. If you exercise on a totally empty stomach, you will feel weak, and even faint. On the other hand, it is a good idea to let at least two hours elapse between eating and exercising. Not only is it very uncomfortable to exercise on a full stomach, and it may even make you feel sick, but the blood, that should be pumping oxygen and glycogen to your muscles, and carrying away carbon dioxide and other waste products, will be diverted to your stomach to help digest your food, and you may well get cramp.

Certainly, the combination of aerobic exercise and diet seems unbeatable when it comes to losing weight. If you diet without exercising, you will lose fat *and* muscle fibre, and of course with less muscle available to burn up fat, it becomes progressively harder to lose weight. With diet and exercise, you not only burn off fat, but increase the amount of muscle available to burn off fat, so losing weight becomes progressively easier.

Exercise and Stress

In recent years, stress has been blamed for a whole range of medical problems, from coronary heart disease, high blood pressure and stomach ulcers to migraine and mental illness. But like so many other things, it's only too much stress that does you harm. If there were no stress at all in your life, you would achieve very little as heart specialist Dr Peter Nixon's 'Human Function Curve' shows only too clearly.

If you're stuck at home with no stress – or arousal or stimulation – then your level of performance – or satisfaction or pleasure – will be very low. Up to a certain point, the more stress you are under, the better your performance will be, and in an ideal

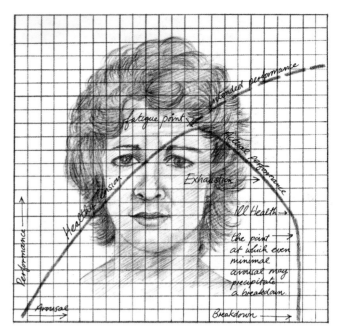

world, you would live on the section of the curve leading up to the peak. Beyond that point, though, further stress will only lead to exhaustion, illness, and ultimately to breakdown.

You can tell when you are over the top and on the downward slope, according to Dr Peter Nixon, by asking yourself a number of questions. Do you, for instance, feel that too much is being demanded of you, and yet find it impossible to say no? Do you feel incompetent, or inadequate? Do you find yourself getting irritable, angry, or impatient with people over trivial things? Do you find it impossible to make decisions, or to remember things, or sort out your priorities? If the answer to all those questions is yes, you are under more stress than is good for you.

To some extent you can control the amount of stress in your life. Doctors have worked out a chart showing how much stress is involved in various events in our lives. Death of a partner is 100, divorce 65, getting married 50, pregnancy 40, moving house 20 and Christmas 12. If the total stress in your life is over 150, you are twice as likely to get ill and if your total is 300, then you are *nine* times as likely to get ill. So if you are pregnant, getting divorced and remarried, then try not to move house at Christmas, too!

What stress does to your body is to set in motion the 'flight or fight' mechanism, built into the human body so that when our ancestors were confronted by a ravenous sabre-toothed tiger, their bodies would be automatically prepared to stand and fight, or to run like hell.

What happens is that you start breathing faster to provide the oxygen your muscles need for action, fat is released into your blood stream for the same reason, and your heart starts beating faster to pump them both to your muscles. Since the blood available in your body is strictly limited, the flight or fight mechanism shuts down other systems that would otherwise need it – digestion, reproduction, and the immune system which fights off disease. The mechanism was designed to deal with short-term, physical stress, so as well as the flight or fight, or 'sympathetic' mechanism, you also have a 'parasympathetic' or 'rest, digest, recover' mechanism which comes into play once the stress is over to make sure your body returns to normal functioning as soon as possible. However, *mental* stress produces the same response in your body, but since this kind of stress – problems at work or at home – tends to last weeks and months rather than days or hours, the 'parasympathetic' mechanism doesn't have a chance to come into operation to restore your body to normal, so it's easy to see why you suffer from chronic indigestion, why your periods become irregular or why you are likely to pick up any bug that's going the rounds.

But in spite of all those drawbacks, it's clear that for some people, stress is addictive, and they go out of their way to seek it. According to Dr Malcolm Carruthers, co-founder of the Positive Health Centre, who has been carrying out research into stress for the last ten years, there is a chemical explanation for it. Under stress, your body produces two chemicals, which set the flight or fight mechanism in motion – adrenaline and noradrenaline. You often hear people talking about something they have enjoyed giving them a 'terrific surge of adrenaline', but Dr Carruthers believes that is inaccurate.

Adrenaline is the fear/anxiety hormone which is produced when you're frightened, embarrassed, or uncertain, and which makes you feel awful. Noradrenaline, on the other hand is the kick-drive hormone, produced when you are in exciting, competitive, aggressive situations. What it does is tickle certain pleasure centres in your brain, making you feel dynamic, sexy, switched on, and generally good about yourself, and relieving depression.

Dr Carruthers found, in the course of his research, that noradrenaline is produced in great quantities by racing drivers during the course of a race, and since intense cold also triggers its production, by the people who leap into the Serpentine, or the English Channel on Christmas Day. Caffeine in coffee also produces it, as does nicotine, which is why, Dr Carruthers believes, many people find it so hard to give up smoking.

Fortunately, exercise also produces noradrenaline, and endorphines, the body's own natural opiates which kill pain, and tickles other pleasure centres in the brain, which is why, although you may be physically exhausted after an exercise session, you feel very good, as though you're on some kind of 'high'. It also explains why some people, who've found it impossible to give up

smoking before, find once they take up regular exercise that they just don't want to smoke any more.

According to Dr Carruthers exercise, and dance especially, is an excellent preventative measure, not just because it burns up the potentially harmful fats that are released when you are under stress, but because it relieves tension, gets you out of your head and into your body, and enables you to express yourself through movement. If you are under some degree of mental stress, and you exercise, then when you stop, your body's 'parasympathetic' system can come into play, overriding your mental state to some extent. But if you are under a lot of stress mentally, and feel exhausted at the end of the day, then you should *not* exercise because the combination of mental and physical stress may well push you over the top of the Human Function Curve, or further down the downward slope, into illness or even breakdown.

Equally, you should not exercise when you are ill, even if you only have a cold, because you would be draining your body's already depleted resources. It is worth remembering that exercise is not a universal panacea; it can make you fitter, but it can't cure you if you are badly run down or ill.

Exercise and Relaxation

You might think that relaxation – another excellent way of coping with stress – is the complete opposite of exercise, but in fact the two things are complementary. In the muscular sense, relaxation is an essential part of movement – unless one set of muscles relaxed as another set contracted, nothing would happen. But in the more general sense, you might think that relaxing, like breathing, is something you do all the time, every time you collapse into a chair or flop into bed. But unfortunately, this is not the case. Next time you think you're relaxed, just check. Are your shoulders all hunched up and your neck muscles tight? Are you gripping the arms of the chair so that your knuckles show white, or tapping your foot unconsciously? And your partner will no doubt be able to tell you if you grind your tightly clenched teeth when you're asleep.

Although relaxation is a mental as well as a physical process, you can approach it, initially anway, as a purely physical technique, and learn how to relax your muscles. As Jane Madders points out in her excellent book, *Stress and Relaxation*, when your muscles are relaxed, it is physically impossible to be in a state of tension. That's not to say that relaxation can take away the *cause* of stress – it can't. But what it can do is alter your response to it, and make you more able to cope with it. Obviously, if you've been exercising regularly, your muscles will be in good shape, so you should find it easy to master the technique of relaxing them, one at a time, starting with your toes, and working up through your whole body.

It's also important to breathe correctly when you're learning to relax. To check if you're breathing properly (i.e. with the lower part of your lungs as well as the upper), put one hand on your abdomen, and one on your chest, and then breathe in. If you are breathing correctly, the hand on your abdomen should move first. Do remember that taking lots of deep breaths will only swamp your breathing centres with oxygen which could actually make you pass out,

and though you could argue that you would certainly be relaxed in that state, there are much safer ways of achieving the desired effect! Once you've mastered the physical techniques, you can move on to deeper relaxation, learning to switch your mind off by picturing a favourite scene or painting, or repeating a word or sound over and over until it becomes meaningless.

It's a good idea to build in a short period of relaxation – five minutes or so – at the end of an exercise class, but the joy of a technique like the one Jane Madders teaches is that you can use it anywhere, anytime, at your office desk, in the kitchen, or even in a traffic jam.

Exercise and Your Back

According to statistics, more working days are lost every year because of back pain than any other single cause. It has been said that the root of the problem lies in the fact that the human body was not designed to walk upright on two legs all the time, but dismissing hundreds and thousands of years of evolution, and crawling round on all fours is hardly a realistic option, so there has to be another solution!

Exercise can help in a number of ways. First, it can strengthen the muscles that support your spine, which makes everything you do – even sitting in a chair – less tiring, and less of a strain. Second, it can make your spine more flexible, and so help prevent the problems that arise from the vertebrae becoming compacted. It can also help improve your posture, and there is no doubt that standing and sitting badly are a major contributory factor in back pain, not to mention headaches and other muscular and nerve pain.

If your posture has been bad most of your life, your muscles will have compensated for it, so that if you have always stood with your head tilted slightly to the right, the muscles on the left side of your neck will be stronger than those on the right. If you start exercising without correcting your posture first, all you will do is compound that distortion.

If you, know your posture is very bad, it might be worth having some lessons in the Alexander Technique before you start your programme of exercise. What this does is make you aware of what you are doing wrong, and teach you how to give instructions to your body to put it right. The technique centres on your spine, teaching you how to expand it lengthways and widthways, and can actually make you an inch taller and an inch broader across your back. It not only improves your posture, and all the problems that spring from it, but also creates more room inside your torso, giving your lungs and other organs more room to function better.

When you are exercising, it is *vitally* important to take care not to injure your back. It's bad enough if you injure any part of your body, but at least under careful supervision, you can exercise round a damaged achilles tendon, or hamstring. If you damage your spine, though, it will affect every single thing you do, even lying in bed!

One fashionable exercise you should *never* do is the double leg lift, where you lie on your back, straighten your legs, and raise them slowly into the air. It not only puts a terrible strain on your lower back and no matter what some teachers may tell you, it is physically impossible to keep your lower back pressed into the floor as you do it) but it also compresses your reproductive organs and your bladder, and what is more it is not even very effective in strengthening the muscles it is meant to strengthen.

Exercise and Pregnancy

Since birth is one of the most physically demanding, athletic events in a woman's life, it makes sense to go into training for it! If you are fit and healthy, your pregnancy will be more comfortable and enjoyable, and the birth itself will probably be easier and less draining, or, as Donna Grant, who has devised her own set of exercises for pregnant women puts it, there'll be less labour in labour. In an ideal world, you will already be exercising before you become pregnant and there is no reason why you can't carry on if you are, or start if you're not, provided of course your doctor says it is safe for you to do so. Most doctors today believe that exercise is good for healthy pregnant women who have no complications, but there are still a few old-fashioned ones who do not approve, so if yours says no, for no apparent reason, then either ask at the anti-natal clinic, or see another doctor.

If you are already attending a class, there is no reason why you shouldn't carry on, provided you tell the teacher you are pregnant so that she can tell you which exercises to avoid. But whether you are carrying on or starting from scratch, your exercise programme will need to take account of your special needs.

The main strain you are likely to feel during pregnancy is on your lower back, which is not surprising since your spine has to adjust to carrying the weight of your growing baby. Fortunately the muscles which support the spine respond very quickly to the right sort of stretching exercises and become stronger, so that with a bit of luck you won't have to suffer backache during pregnancy. Obviously, the way you stand and sit when you are pregnant makes a big difference to your back. What you should aim to do is keep your shoulders and hips in a straight line, which involves tightening your buttocks and tilting your pelvis slightly forward. That way, your pelvis and buttocks are supporting the weight of your upper body, and your lower back is lengthened which prevents it curving inwards to take the strain of the baby's weight, and giving you backache.

When you sit down, try not to sink back in the chair. If you do, the baby will be pressing on major nerves and organs, stopping them from working properly. Ideally, you should sit with your back straight, and you might find it easier to sit

cross-legged on the floor, with your back against the wall. Sitting in that position also involves the 'passive' stretching of the muscles in your thighs and groin, which will also help during the birth.

Another very important area to concentrate on is your abdomen. As the baby grows, it fills up that space, so the aim of exercising the 'abdomenal corset' as it's called, is to make the muscles stronger and more elastic, thereby creating more space, which is better for the baby and more comfortable for you.

Standing properly also helps strengthen these muscles. If you stand badly, allowing your lower back to take the strain, then your abdomenal muscles will sag, and it will be much harder work to get them back into shape after the birth. Whether you're sitting or standing, try and keep as much distance as you can between your pelvis and your rib cage, and don't let the upper part of your body sink down onto your sac.

A group of muscles you are probably not even aware that you own are the pelvic floor muscles, which actually push the baby out when the time comes. In their book, *Exercises for Childbirth*, Barbara Dale and Johanna Roeber describe a simple way of identifying those muscles and seeing how strong they are. When you're emptying your bladder, try and cut off the flow completely, though obviously do make sure you go on to empty it completely afterwards. The muscles you are using are the pelvic floor and if you can stop the flow, then they are pretty strong. If you cannot, then practice contracting and relaxing the muscles now you know where they are, an exercise you can do anytime, anywhere, even standing in a bus queue! If you make those muscles stronger and learn to control them, it will pay dividends during the birth. Labour will probably be quicker and easier, and getting the baby out as fast as possible means there is less risk of it suffering trauma in the birth canal. Since the muscles are more elastic, there is less chance that you'll have to have an episiotomy, but if you do, or if you tear during the birth, the muscles should heal more easily.

There is no reason why you should not carry on exercising right up the start of labour if you feel up to it, though you may find in the last few weeks that all you want to do is rest and sleep. Listen to your body, it will tell you what it wants to do, and that is another reason why exercise during pregnancy is a good idea. It makes you aware of your body and helps you to realise that you are not ill – a view which too many members of the medical profession still hold – or helpless. Equally important, it makes you feel in control of your body, a useful antidote to the sensation many women feel during pregnancy of being 'taken over'.

After birth, exercise can help you get back into shape very quickly. You can start doing *very gentle* exercises to help your womb shrink back to its former size about ten days after the birth. During the first few months, you are likely to feel exhausted a lot of the time, what with breast feeding, and broken nights, but you should try and get back to your exercise class within three months if you can, because if you leave it much longer, your body will get used to its new size and shape, and it will be much harder work. With all the demands on your time, it's not easy to fit in an exercise class, but it is well worth making the effort because not only does exercise produce a natural 'high', but also the fact that you see your body getting back into shape is a great boost to your morale.

Starting Exercise

Whatever programme of exercise you decide to do, a number of basic rules apply. First make sure the room in which you are working is airy and warm, and that you wear warm clothing because if you are cold, your whole body feels tight, and you are much more likely to damage a muscle. It's something that professional dancers understand only too well – a damaged muscle can be disastrous for their careers – which is why most of them look like scarecrows during class, dressed in a motley assortment of leotards, tracksuits, sweaters, over-trousers, legwarmers and even woolly scarves!

If you wear a leotard and tights, then until you are thoroughly warm, wear a tracksuit or sweatshirt over the top. Natural fibres like cotton and wool are better than man-made fibres because they are

warmer and they absorb sweat. If you want to wear legwarmers, remember that their purpose is to warm the muscles of your whole leg, so worn concertina'd round your ankles, they are a fun fashion accessory, but not a lot more!

Every exercise class should contain at least four main elements:

1. Warm-up

This is absolutely essential for *any* form of exercise – even jogging – because muscles that are cold and tight are much more likely to get damaged. Your warm up should start with some gentle stretching exercises to loosen up your muscles, some mobilising exercises (gentle twisting movements) to get your joints and muscles ready for more strenuous work later on, and some gentle aerobics, jogging on the spot for a few minutes, say, just to get your heart and lungs ready for work.

The amount of time you spend warming up depends on the temperature in the room – the colder it is, the longer it will take, but it should not last more than five minutes. If a particular group of muscles feel tight and stiff, then work on it until it loosens up. If it doesn't, then avoid working on it strenuously that day.

2. Aerobics

These exercises – jogging or running on the spot, doing star jumps, or twisting jumps – are designed to get your heart and lungs working hard, and should last about twelve minutes to give you the full benefit. But do remember that you should be breathing hard at the end, not gasping for breath, so if you reach that point three, or seven minutes into that section, then stop. As you get fitter, you will be able to carry on longer.

3. Improving Muscle Strength and Muscle Tone

These exercises involve working on particular groups of muscles – arms, stomachs, thighs, bottoms, calves and so on – gradually building up their strength and improving their tone by repetition.

4. Cool down

It is only quite recently that the importance of a cool down period at the end of an exercise session has been generally realised. The aim is to let your pulse rate return gradually to normal. While you've been exercising hard, blood has been pumped to all your extremities, so if you just stop suddenly, there may not be enough blood immediately available to your brain, so you could feel dizzy.

Cooling down also helps ward off post-exercise stiffness in your muscles. Again, if you just stop abruptly, muscles that have been working hard are likely to stiffen up and hurt, so it's a good idea to do some passive stretching at the end of a class too, just to pull the muscles out to their fullest extent.

Part 3
THE CLASSES

Are you ready to put it all into practice? We've devised five very varied programmes for you to try, prepared under the guidance of some of our top teachers. They are demonstrated by professional dancers and even the teachers themselves, to ensure complete clarity, so don't worry if you cannot achieve the same standards yourself – you're doing it for enjoyment, not to compete. Before you start, do read my list of basic rules – they will help you to develop the right attitude towards exercising!

Take it from Here!

1

Try to make a realistic habit of exercising. Don't make impossible demands on yourself which you know you just won't be able to meet. Obviously a little exercise every day would be an ideal to aim for, but two or three times a week, using a programme that suits you and makes the right sort of demands on your body and time, is better than none at all.

2

Try to avoid 'habits' when exercising. As you get to know a particular programme it should become easier for you, but don't make that an excuse for not trying harder. When you feel ready, move on to another programme.

3

Put some music on. This works wonders and helps to put you in the right frame of mind. I think you should make your own choice, but try to find something that bears some relation to the exercise you are doing.

4

Wear something loose, warm and sensible. A tracksuit or leotard and some legwarmers would be ideal.

5

Be sensible about what you eat, especially if you are on a diet to lose weight. An extra knee-bend in the morning does not mean you qualify for pudding at lunchtime!

6

If, like most of us, you find it hard to be inspired on your own, try and get your partner or a friend involved. Apart from the mutual benefits, it's more fun with two!

7

Take a positive attitude! Be honest with yourself and try to 'think health'. In a few weeks time everything will feel firmer and look better. You could well be taking on a whole new lease of life.

8

A regular routine means taking the 'whole' approach: not just regular exercise but taking care about what you eat and drink as well. If you need advice, consult your doctor.

9

Make sure you are in a reasonable state of fitness before you start any of the more rigorous routines that follow. If you are under medical supervision or taking medication, if you are pregnant or just plain out-of-condition, once again, do consult your doctor first.

10

Lastly, don't forget to make it fun! Dancing is about many things, but I think it's the best non-competitive sport there is. Enjoy it!

Kay Cornelius
AEROBICS

The value of an aerobics class is that it is going to make your heart and lungs work better. What you have to do to achieve this is to follow the routine carefully, and take your pulse whenever indicated by the heart symbol – five times in all. If you are uncertain how to check your pulse, turn back to page 62. Your aim is to raise the pulse rate into your target training zone, which means that you have to get your heart working harder – but not too hard! To work out your target zone, refer to the chart below. Everybody has a maximum pulse rate, and to calculate yours, simply subtract your age from 220, and take off an additional 40 if you consider yourself very unfit. This is then your *maximum* pulse rate, and you should make sure you never exceed 85 per cent of this number. However, to benefit from the arobic programme, you must aim to reach the 70 per cent level. Check carefully before you start exercising, so you are quite sure exactly what pulse rates are correct for you.

The class itself is divided into five separate sections: warm-up, aerobics, cool-down, calisthenics and final cool-down. It is structured to ensure that you not only exercise vigorously, but that you also stretch and condition your muscles as well – so follow the exercises exactly in the sequence shown.

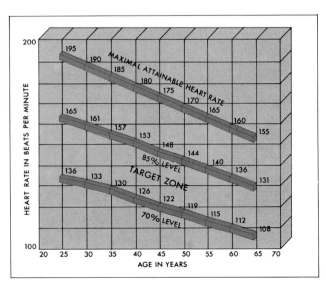

Before you begin . . . remember . . .

Take your pulse rate 5 times:
1 Resting rate (before you start): a normal person's is around 72 beats per minute, though an athlete's will be much lower.
2 After the warm up: you should not yet be in your target training zone – if you are, then during the aerobics section only pick your feet up gently.
3 After the aerobic section: check to see if you're within the target zone, and adjust your effort accordingly next time.
4 After the cool-down: if your pulse is still over 120 at this stage, you have been exercising too vigorously, and must take it more gently next time.
5 At the end of the final cool-down: if your heart has not returned to its resting rate, allow yourself a few minutes more to recover before you get up.

Some of the exercises are recommended for advanced students only (A), and while it isn't always easy to know how to classify yourself to start with, you are certainly a beginner (B) if you haven't been taking any regular exercise for several years. As you become fitter, and your heart more efficient, your pulse will be lower as every beat will be a stronger beat. The pulse is an unbeatable lie-detector, and you can use it to guide you as to when you should attempt the advanced programme. It may well take several months, or even longer, but whatever level you attempt, you will see improvement if you persevere.

Wear sensible shoes for the aerobic section itself, and avoid those with a high back as this can cause irritation to the achilles tendons.

Some of the exercises are divided into sets, for example the instruction may read 'repeat 3 sets of 8'. You could of course count on up to 24, but it makes it a lot easier, and develops a sense of rhythm, if you break the counting into sets.

Warm-up

Exercise 1: to stretch your sides, hamstrings, legs
Stand with your feet about 18 inches apart, pointing slightly outwards, arms by your sides.

Stretch up with your right arm, fingers extended, at the same time bending your right knee, raising your right heel and pressing the ball of your right foot into the floor. Repeat to the left.
Repeat 8 times on each side B/A

From the same starting position, raise your right arm and stretch over to the left, making sure your torso is square on to the front, and bounce gently.
Repeat 8 times on each side B/A

With your feet in the same position, bend forward from the waist, keeping your back flat, bend your knees then swing your arms through your legs and out again, stretching them in front of you with your back flat.
Repeat 8 times B/A

Exercise 2: for abdomen, waist, back, hamstrings and shoulders

Stand with your feet about 12 inches apart, pointing slightly outwards and your arms straight out to the sides. Swing down and grab your left ankle (or calf, if you can't reach) with your right hand, put your left arm straight up in the air, and pull yourself in.
Repeat 4 times B/8 times A
Repeat the move, holding onto your right ankle, then come to the centre, and holding both ankles, pull yourself down.
Repeat 4 times B/8 times A

Exercise 3 (Advanced only): to stretch hamstrings and spine

Stand with your feet about 24 inches apart and parallel, with your arms at your sides. Bend forward from the waist, pushing your bottom out to hollow your lower spine, stretch your arms to the sides, and bounce gently. Bending your knees, swing your arms through your legs as far as they will go, and out again, straightening your knees and hollowing your back.
Repeat 3 times

Exercise 4: to stretch calf muscles and achilles tendons

Stand with your feet together, arms by your sides. Bend from your waist, keeping your legs straight. Put the palms of your hands on the floor, and 'walk' them away from your feet until your heels can hardly stay on the floor any longer. Bend your right knee so that heel comes right off the floor, then as you straighten your right knee, making sure your right heel is firmly back on the floor, bend your left knee. Alternate for 8 counts.
Repeat 4 times B/A

Aerobics

Exercise 1
Jog on the spot,
making sure that
each heel is flat
on the floor
every time that
the foot comes
down, for a
count of 8.
Repeat: 3 sets of 8 B/A

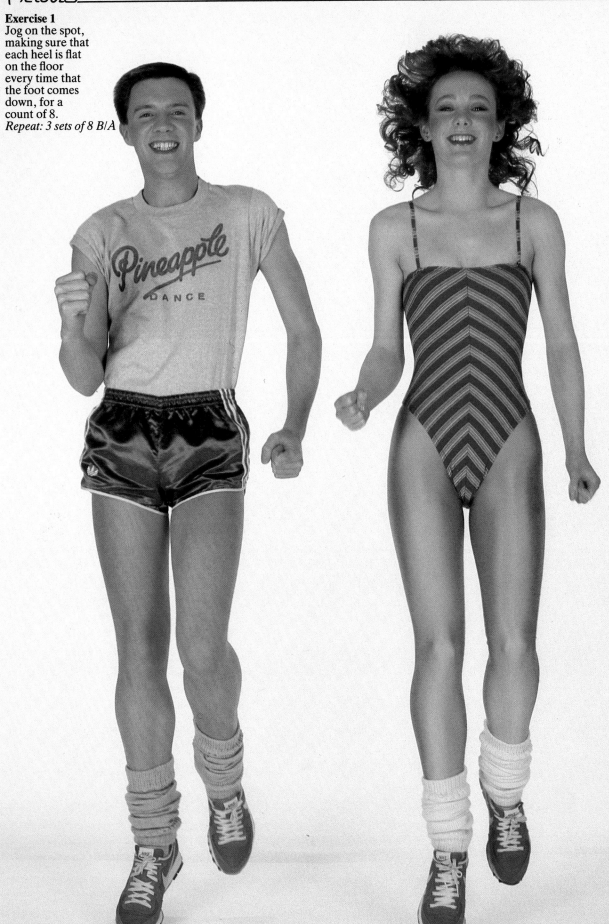

Exercise 2
With your hands on your waist and your feet about 12 inches apart, hop on the spot, bouncing on your left foot for 2 counts as you kick your right foot out in front of you, then bouncing on your right for 2 counts, kicking with your left. Alternate for 8 counts in all.
Repeat: 3 sets of 8 B/A

Exercise 3
From the same starting position, bounce on your right foot as you kick your left leg out to the side. Bring your left foot back in front of your right, then bounce on that foot as you kick your right leg out to the side – just like the sailors' hornpipe. Alternate for 8 counts.
Repeat: 3 sets of 8 B/A

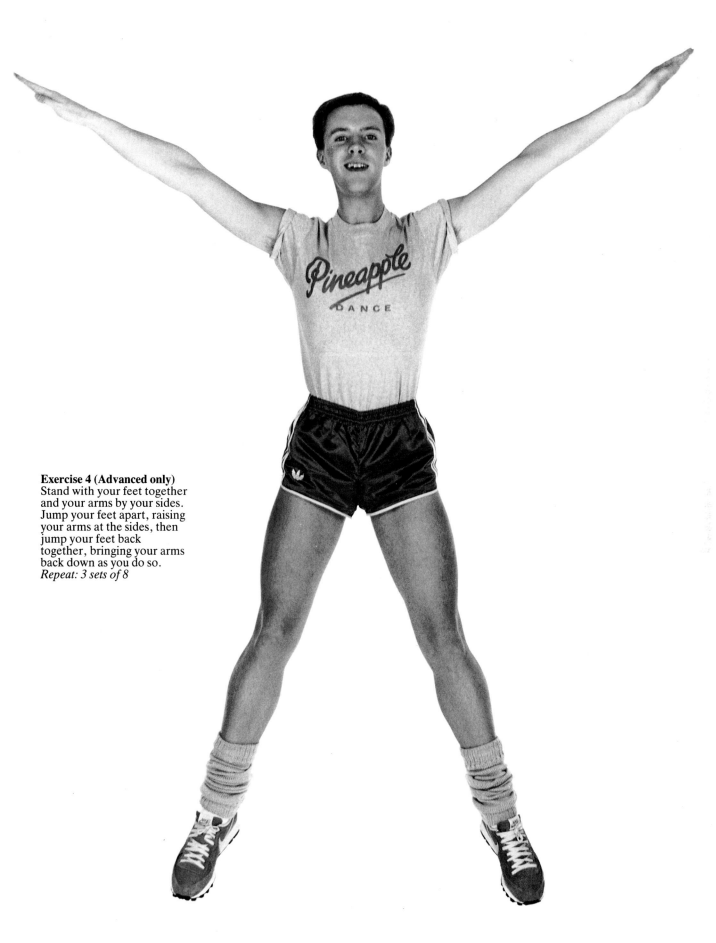

Exercise 4 (Advanced only)
Stand with your feet together
and your arms by your sides.
Jump your feet apart, raising
your arms at the sides, then
jump your feet back
together, bringing your arms
back down as you do so.
Repeat: 3 sets of 8

Exercise 5 (Advanced only)
Stand with your feet
together, your knees bent,
both pointing to the left, and
both arms stretched out to
the right. As you jump just
an inch or two off the floor,

swing your arms and legs in
opposite directions, so that
you land with your feet and
knees pointing to the right,
and your arms to the left.
Repeat: 3 set of 8

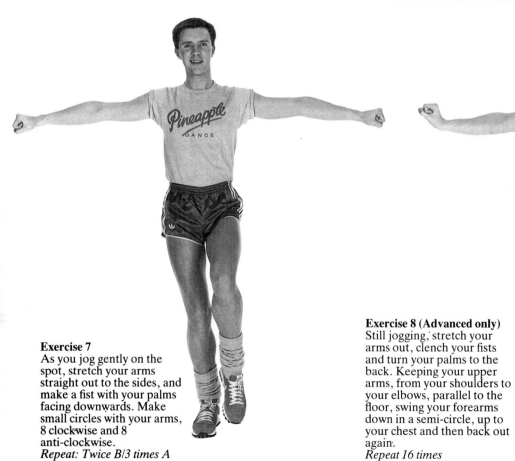

Exercise 7
As you jog gently on the
spot, stretch your arms
straight out to the sides, and
make a fist with your palms
facing downwards. Make
small circles with your arms,
8 clockwise and 8
anti-clockwise.
Repeat: Twice B/3 times A

Exercise 8 (Advanced only)
Still jogging, stretch your
arms out, clench your fists
and turn your palms to the
back. Keeping your upper
arms, from your shoulders to
your elbows, parallel to the
floor, swing your forearms
down in a semi-circle, up to
your chest and then back out
again.
Repeat 16 times

Exercise 6 (Advanced only)
Stand with your feet about 12 inches apart, your forearms bent up to your shoulders. As you bounce twice on your left foot, bring your right knee up to touch your left elbow. Then bounce twice on your right foot and try to bring your left up to your right elbow.
Repeat: 3 sets of 8

Aerobic cool-down

Exercise 1
As Warm-up Exercise 1.

Exercise 2
Stand with your legs about 18 inches apart, then flop forward from the waist, holding on to your left ankle; hold for 4 counts pulling yourself in.
Then swing across to your right ankle, and pull yourself towards your knee, hold for 4 counts, then back to the centre, and holding both ankles, pull yourself in for 4 counts.
Repeat: 3 times

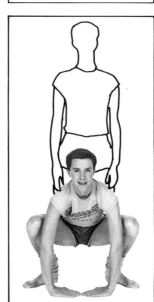

Exercise 3
Stand with your feet 18 inches apart, pointing outwards. Bend your knees, put the palms of your hands flat on the floor, and press your elbows into the sides of your knees, gently bouncing your bottom down towards the floor. Stretch both legs and repeat sequence.
Repeat: 3 times

Calisthenics

Exercise 1: for buttocks, hips, thighs and stomach
Kneel on the floor, keeping your back flat, then swing your right leg, with the knee still bent, out to the side, as high as it

will comfortably go. Try to keep your hips straight, and don't put all your weight onto your left side. Swing the leg back, but don't let it touch the ground. *Repeat: 3 sets of 8 B/A*

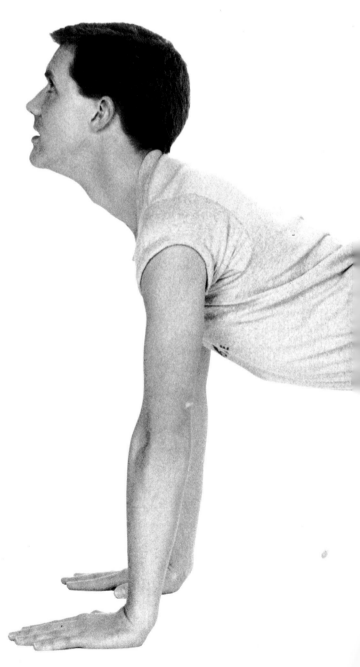

Exercise 2: for hips, thighs, legs and spine
Kneel on the floor, then bring your left knee in towards your chest, rounding your spine and tucking your bottom in. Swing your left leg straight out behind you as high as it will comfortably go, lifting your head and stretching your spine. *Repeat: 2 sets of 8 each side B/A*

Exercise 3: for hips and legs
Sit cross-legged with your back straight.
Stretch your arms straight out at the sides, then lean forward
from the waist as far as you can, place your hands on the
floor, and let your head drop forward. Relax into this
position. Straighten up, keeping your back straight.

Exercise 4 (Advanced only): for inner and outer thighs
Lie on your left side, supporting yourself on your left forearm, with both palms flat on the floor.

Bring your right knee into your chest, straighten it again, then lift it into the air as high as you can, and return it to the starting position. *Repeat: 4 sets of 8 each side*

Exercise 5 (Advanced only): for inner thighs
Lie on your left side, supporting yourself on your left forearm. Bend your right leg and put your right foot in front of your left knee, holding onto the ankle with your right hand. Keeping your inner thigh facing the ceiling, raise and lower your left leg a few inches.
Repeat: 18 times each side with your foot pointed, and 18 with it flexed.

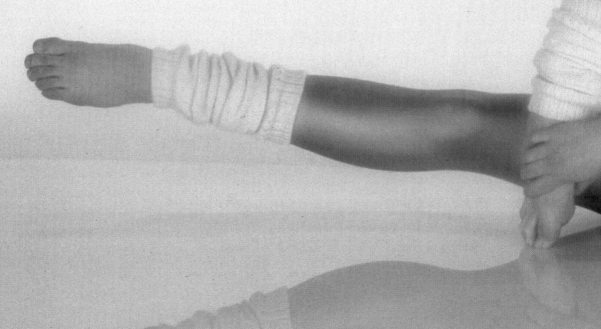

Exercise 6: for legs
Sit on the floor, keeping your back straight, put the soles of your feet together and pull them as close to your body as you can. Hold onto your feet with both hands, and bounce your knees gently outwards, down towards the floor for 16 counts.

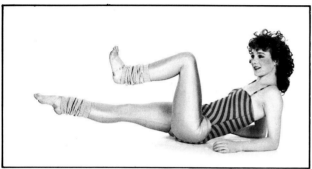

Exercise 7: for stomach muscles
Lie on your back, supporting your weight on your elbows, and push your lower back firmly into the floor.
'Bicycle' with your legs, pointing your feet as you stretch your legs out, and flexing them as you bend them in again.
Repeat 16 times B/24 times A

For the Advanced version, put your hands behind your head, elbows out to the sides, and lift your shoulders off the floor as you 'bicycle'.

Exercise 8 (Advanced only): for stretching the spine and stomach muscles
Lie on your back with your knees bent, your hips raised, your feet about 12 inches apart, and your hands, palms down, on either side of your head.
Push up with your arms into a back bend, and return to the floor.
Repeat once

 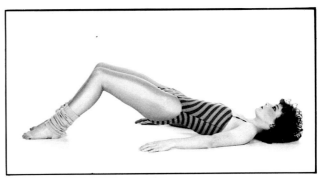

Exercise 9: for your bottom
Lie on your back, knees bent, feet in line with your hips, hands by your sides. Push your bottom up so that your shoulders are supporting your weight, and your body is a straight line from knees to chest. Raise and lower your bottom just a few inches, squeezing your buttocks as tight as you can. If you're doing it properly there should be no strain in your back. *Repeat: 20 times B/50 times A*

Exercise 10: for hips, legs, abdomen and back
Bend from the waist, put both hands on the floor. Bend your right leg and stretch your left leg out behind you, with both heels off the floor. Bounce gently 8 times. You should feel the stretch down the back of your left leg.
Then put your right knee on the floor, under your body, lower your left knee to the floor and reaching behind you with your right hand, grab the toes of your left foot.
Try to pull that foot away, so you feel the stretch in your arm, your leg, your back and diagonally across your abdomen.
Hold it for a count of 4, then repeat the other side.

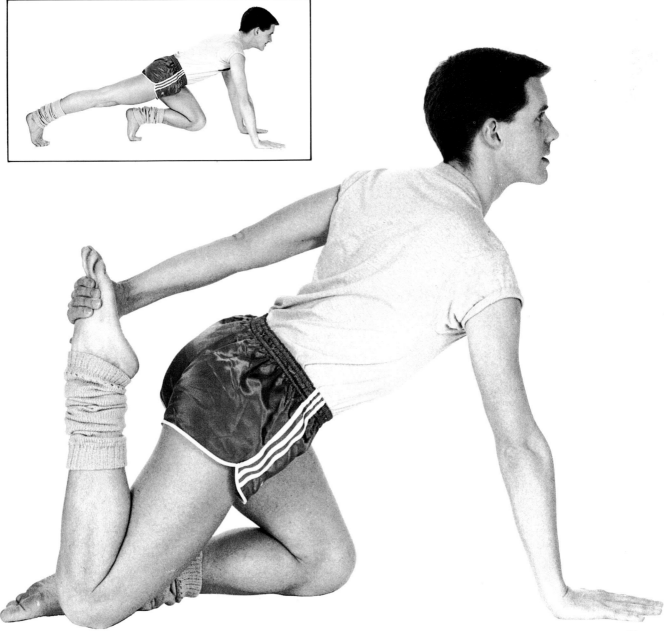

Final cool-down

Exercise 1: for inner thigh, waist and lower spine
Sit on the floor, your legs stretched as wide apart as they will comfortably go, toes pointed and your arms above your head.
Stretch over to the left, keeping your torso square on to the front. Swing your right arm over to the right, leaning forward so that your chest is parallel to the floor, then straighten up and stretch over to the right.

Exercise 2: to stretch and relax your spine
Kneel on the floor with your knees slightly apart. Push your bottom up and lift your head, so that your spine is stretched.

Slowly round your back, pushing your chin in towards your chest. Hold it for a count of 4 and slowly return to your starting position.

Exercise 3
Lie flat on your back, legs slightly apart, arms away from your sides, palms up, and chin at right-angles to the floor. Concentrate on relaxing every muscle in your body, starting at your toes and winding up with your forehead and scalp. Try and empty your mind of all thoughts for a minute or two, and enjoy the feeling of being at one with yourself and your body.

Arlene Phillips
JAZZ

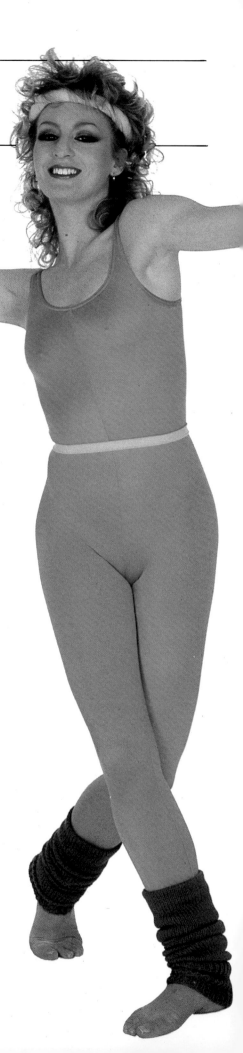

What you will see over the next few pages are some of the exercises I and my assistants teach in the jazz dance classes at Pineapple. There are stretch and dance exercises, then a short routine which we learn for the last part of the class . . . over a few classes these little routines might build up into a sequence of steps, or a new dance.

Study the photographs and check in the mirror to see that you are in the right positions every time. Don't expect to be as perfect as the girl here, though! She's my assistant Dominique, and it's taken her a lot of practice to reach this level.

Start by wearing something loose and comfortable, and leave the feet bare. Do your exercises in a warm room, since you need to keep those muscles warm as you work. And don't start the routine straight after a heavy meal . . . leave it at least two hours before you begin.

The time you choose is up to you. I prefer to exercise after a day's work because I find it really sets me up for the evening, but you might want to do it early in the morning or during your lunch break. Then try to build up a regular programme of three times a week.

The first time you try these exercises at home, you might feel a bit stiff. That's a sign that you have been working those muscles. Take a hot bath and relax and the pain should go away. (Of course, see your doctor if you are suffering badly.) Don't strain under any circumstances. Do the routine well, and try pushing yourself just a little bit further than you think you can go! You have nothing to lose but your pounds.

Exercise 1

1 Stand with your feet wide apart, pointing outwards.
2 Raise your arms above your head, and stretching up with your left arm, bend your left knee and shift your weight onto it. Stretch up with your right arm, and repeat twice.
3 Straighten your legs and put your arms above your head.

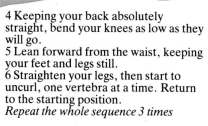

4 Keeping your back absolutely straight, bend your knees as low as they will go.
5 Lean forward from the waist, keeping your feet and legs still.
6 Straighten your legs, then start to uncurl, one vertebra at a time. Return to the starting position.
Repeat the whole sequence 3 times

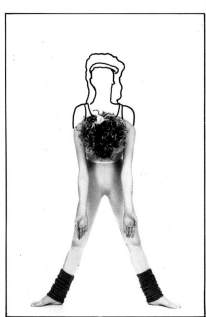

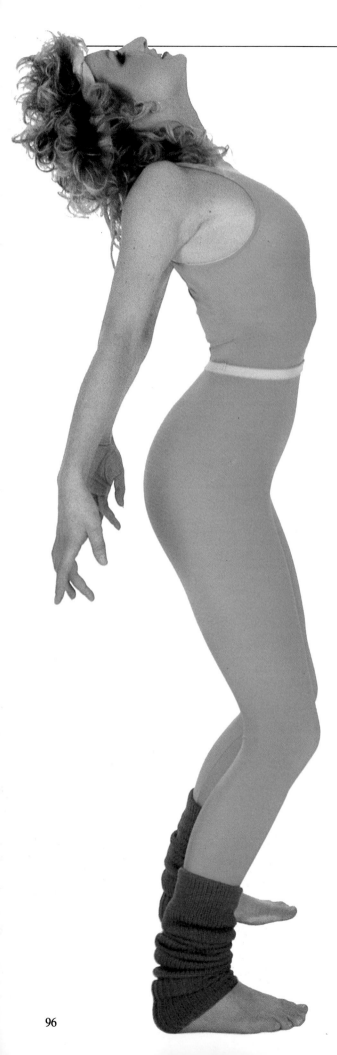

Exercise 2

1 Stand with your feet shoulder-width apart and parallel.
2 Bend your knees, stick your bottom out, try and pull your shoulder-blades together, and let your head drop back (see left).
3 Bend forward from the waist, keeping your shoulder-blades pulled together and your head up, and hollow your lower back. You should feel the pull down the backs of your thighs.
4 Keeping your knees bent, lean forward from the waist, and touch the floor with the palms of your hands.
5 Straighten your knees, and uncurl one vertebra at a time.
Repeat 8 times

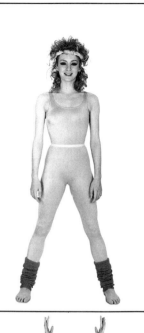

Exercise 3

1 Stand with your feet wide apart, pointing outwards, and your arms above your head.
2 Stretch over to the right, making sure that your torso stays square on to the front and that your right shoulder doesn't move forward.
3 Twist at the waist so that your chest is parallel to the floor, and keep your back absolutely straight.
4 Pull yourself down over your right leg, then swing across to the left, (5) and (6), and reversing the order of movements 3, 2 and 1, return to your starting position (9).
Repeat, starting to the left.

Exercise 4

1 Stand with your feet together, pointing outwards, and your arms straight out to the sides.

2 Bring your hands in to your chest, and as you bend your knees, keeping your back absolutely straight (3), move your hands in an arc down to your waist and out to the sides.

4 As you carry on bending your knees, you'll find that your heels will come off the floor.

5 Keeping your back straight and your arms out to the sides, slowly straighten up, putting your heels back on the floor as soòn as you physically can.
Repeat 4 times

Exercise 4a

Stand with your feet shoulder-width apart, pointing outwards, and repeat Exercise 4, *keeping your heels on the floor throughout.*
Repeat 4 times

98

Exercise 5
Stand with your feet about 18 inches apart, and parallel, then
'walk' them as far forward as you can *without your heels
coming off the floor*. You should feel the stretch right down
the backs of your legs.
Repeat once

Exercise 6
Stand with your feet wide apart, pointing outwards, with your arms stretched out to the sides. Keeping your hips absolutely still, move the upper part of your body to the left, then back to the centre again.
Repeat: alternate to R and L 4 times

Exercise 6a (opposite)
Stand with your feet about 18 inches apart, and parallel, knees bent, elbows tucked into your waist and hands out to the side. Swing your pelvis to the left, so that your hip hits your elbow, back to the centre, and then repeat to the right.
Repeat 4 times

Exercise 6b
Stand in the same position as for Exercise 6a. Tilt your pelvis forward, then back to the centre. Stick your bottom out, hollowing your lower back, then back to the centre.
Repeat 4 times

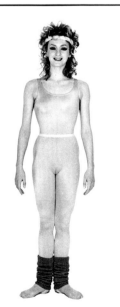

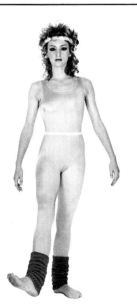

Exercise 7
Stand with your legs together, feet pointing outwards, with your arms by your sides. Extend your right leg in front of you and lift it about 6 inches off the floor. Draw a circle in the air with your right foot, 4 times clockwise and 4 times anti-clockwise.
Repeat with the other foot

Exercise 8
Sit on the floor, back straight, and feet flexed (pointing to the ceiling).
Bend forward, holding your ankles or calves, pulling your chest down over your knees as far as you can comfortably go, and point your toes. You should feel the stretch in the back of your legs and in your ankles.
Repeat 4 times

Exercise 9 (above)
Lie on the floor, propped up on your elbows with your toes pointed. Bend your right knee up, then straighten the leg into the air as close to a right-angle with the floor as you can manage. *Repeat 4 times with each leg*

Exercise 9a (right)
Repeat the exercise with both legs together. *Repeat 4 times*

Exercise 10 (below)
Lie flat on the floor with your toes pointed.
Lift your right leg to as near a right-angle with the floor as you can manage, then swing it straight out to the right as far as it will comfortably go without lifting your bottom off the floor, then bring it back to the starting position.
Repeat 4 times with each leg

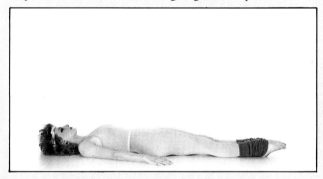

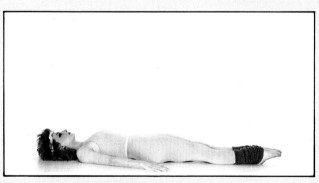

Exercise 11
Sit on the floor with your
back straight, your legs
stretched out as far as they
will comfortably go and your
arms out to the side.

Stretch over to the left,
keeping your torso square on
to the front.
Bend forward from the
waist, stretching your arms
out to the sides, so that your
chest is parallel to the floor.
Straighten up and stretch
over to the right, then return

to your starting position.
Repeat starting to the right.
Repeat 4 times

Exercise 12
Stand with your feet shoulder-width apart and parallel, with your arms by your sides. Keeping your shoulders back, let your head drop forward, return it to the centre, then let it fall back.

With your chin parallel to the floor, turn your head to the left, then to the right, making sure you keep your shoulders quite still.
Repeat 4 times

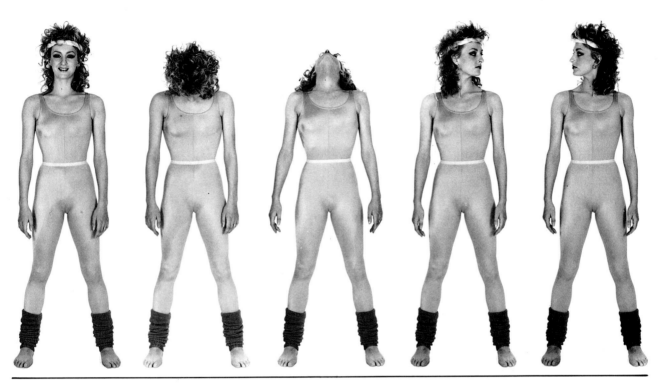

Exercise 13
Stand in the same position as for Exercise 12.
Make circles with your shoulders by rolling them forward, trying to pull them up to your ears, pushing them down and back before returning to your starting position. *Repeat 4 times*

Exercise 13a
Repeat the previous exercise, only this time, bend your knees as you roll your shoulders forward, and straighten them as you pull them up and back.
Repeat 4 times

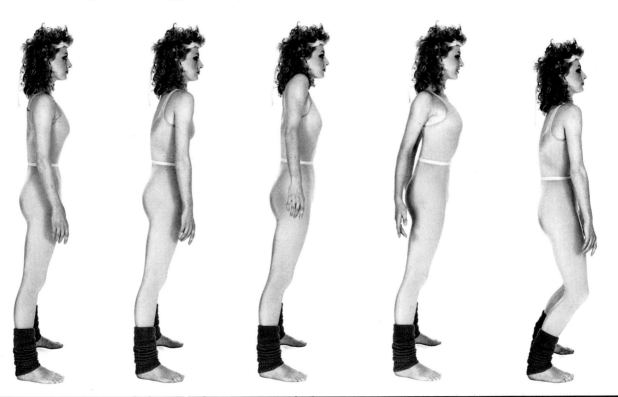

Exercise 14
Stand with your feet together
and parallel, and your arms
above your head.
Bend your knees and make
matching circles with your
arms and hips.
If you find it hard to
co-ordinate the movements
at first, try it slowly:
arms/hips out to the left-to
the front-to the right-to the
back.
*Repeat 4 times clockwise and
4 times anti-clockwise*

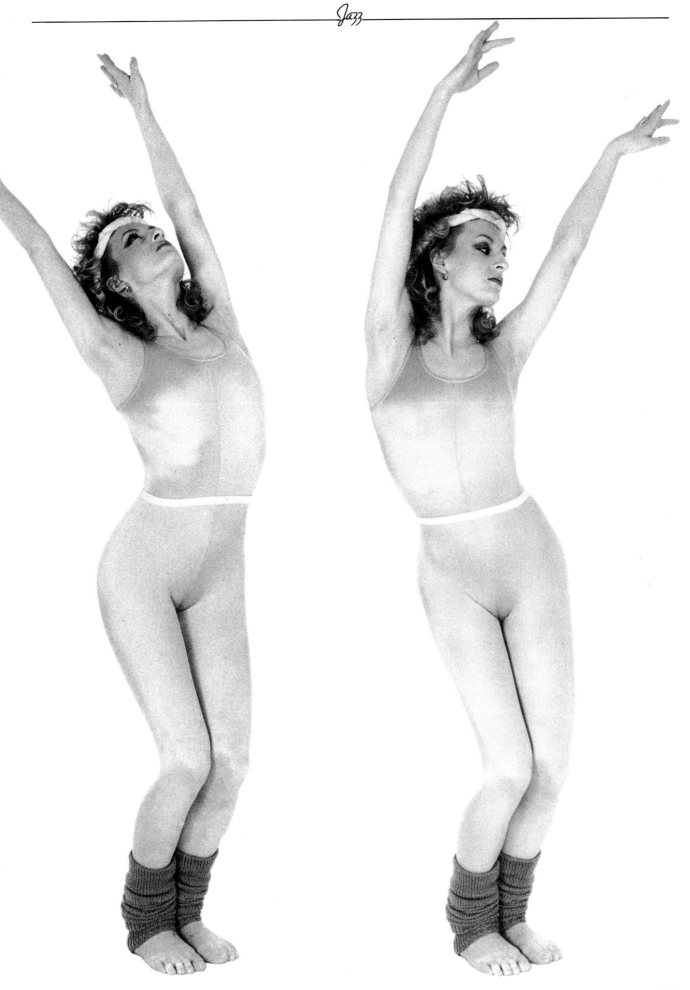

Routine

To be done to a count of 8

(A) On ONE, put your left foot about 18 inches in front of the right, bend your knees, tilt your left hip up, and keep your torso square on to the front. On the 'AND' (one-AND-two) swing your pelvis back and, on TWO, forward again.

(B) On THREE, keep your feet still, and turn your torso so that your back is facing the front, at the same time swinging your arms in, so that your hands cross in front of you and out again.
(C) On FOUR, return to your starting position, repeating the same movement with your hands.
(D) On FIVE, bring your right leg across in front of your left, and bring your hands up to your shoulders.
(E) On the 'AND' (five-AND-six), step across to the left with your left leg, so that you are standing with your feet apart.
(F) On SIX, bring your right leg across behind your left, bending your right knee, and stretch your arms straight up.
(G) On SEVEN, stretch your arms straight out to the sides, then roll your right shoulder forward.
(H) on EIGHT, roll your left shoulder forward.
Repeat the routine, starting with your right foot

A

F

E

F

C

D

G

H

Michael King
BODY CONTROL

You don't need to be a professional dancer to recognise Body Control as an extremely effective way for everyone to keep the body toned, stretched and healthy. What we teach is based on the Pilates Method, which was originally devised specially to help injured dancers, but now adapted to help absolutely anybody to isolate and exercise specific parts of the body. And the joy of this method is that it's gentle and slow . . . no rushing about.

The only major difference between the exercises I have devised for you to try at home and those we teach in the studio is that at Pineapple we can also show you how to use the special equipment and body reformer machines. At home, though, all you need is to get down on the carpet: you don't need anything else you wouldn't already have around the house.

To start with, I have demonstrated some general posture exercises, a shoulder exercise to do with a broom handle, and then a stretch programme that you can do either on your own or with a partner.

Go as far as you can with each exercise and just watch your own progress. It is disciplined, but it's fun too!

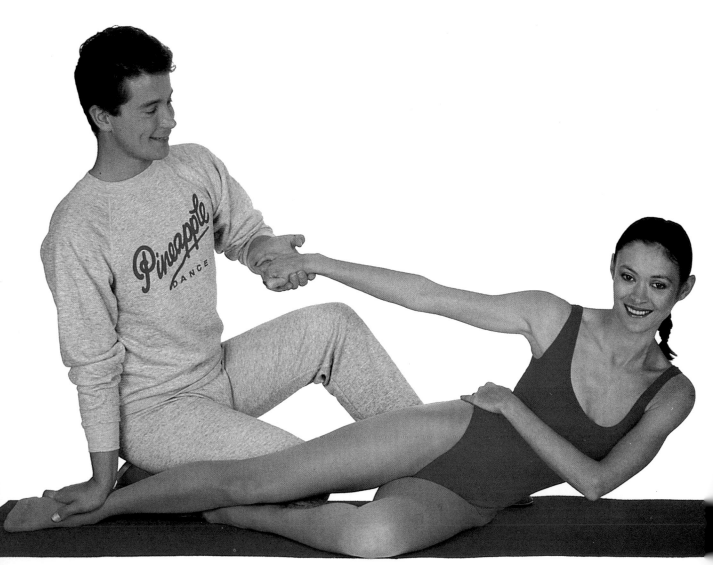

Incorrect

Correct

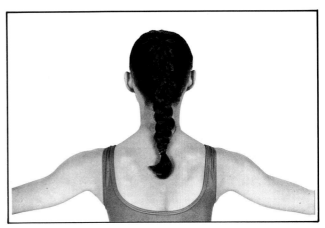

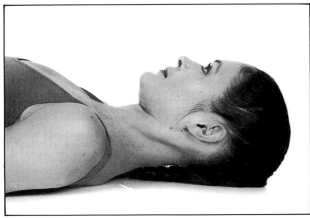

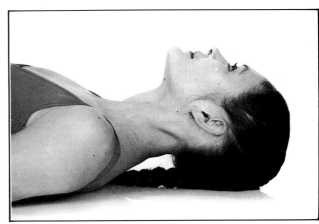

Before you start the exercises, it is very important to make sure that your posture is correct. If it isn't then the exercises won't do you any good, and could even do you harm. Using these photographs check the alignment of your back, neck and shoulders and try to relax into the correct posture.

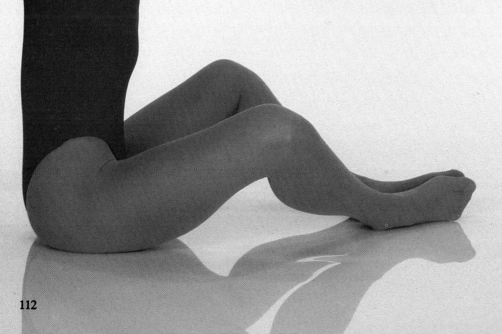

Exercise 1

Sit with your knees bent, the soles of your feet together, your back straight and your arms in the air. If you suffer from tension in your shoulders, try the alternative starting position shown above, doing the exercise with your hands crossed behind your head. Bounce gently forward from your waist to stretch out your lower spine.
Repeat 16 times

Exercise 2
Point your toes and stretch your legs so hard that your heels come off the floor, then bounce gently forward from the waist.
Repeat 16 times

Exercise 3
This time, flex your feet, stretch your legs hard and bounce from the waist as before.
Repeat 16 times

Exercise 4
Keeping your right leg stretched out in front of you, bend your left leg and press the sole of your left foot against the inside of your right knee, and bounce gently forward from the waist.
Repeat 16 times R, 16 times L

Exercise 5
Sitting in the same position as for the previous exercise turn the body to face the bent knee and bounce gently over to the right, keeping your left arm well back and your right arm parallel with your right leg. You should feel the stretch all down your left side.
Repeat 16 times R, 16 times L

113

Exercise 6
For this exercise you will need a pole about 4 feet long or failing that a towel, though you must keep it taut throughout the exercise. Stand with your feet about 18 inches apart, pointing outwards, your back straight, your stomach pulled in. Hold the pole with your hands widely spaced.
The aim is to take the pole virtually in a circle, from the front of your body to the back in one smooth movement; keep your arms straight throughout. As your shoulders become looser, you will be able to move your hands closer together on the pole.
Repeat 8 times

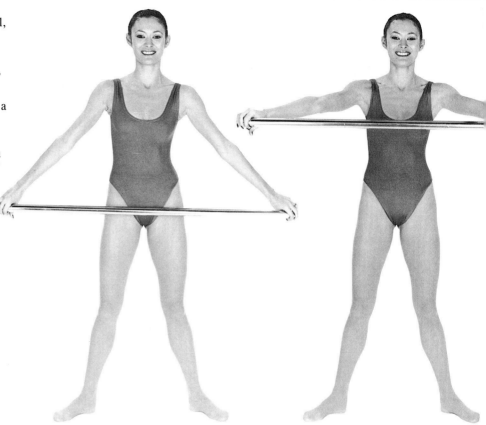

Exercise 7
Kneel on the floor, your back straight. Swing your right knee in towards your chest, then swing it out again, extending your right leg as high as it will go behind you. Bring it into your chest again without returning to the starting position.
Repeat 16 times R, 16 times L

Exercise 8: for thigh muscles
1 Lie on your back, your knees bent, and the soles of your feet flat on the floor. Put a cushion or a pillow between your knees and squeeze them together as hard as you can. Hold for a count of 10. (Do make sure your neck muscles aren't taking the strain – check posture photograph.)
Repeat 5 times
2 In the advanced version – for stomach muscles as well as thighs – raise your head and shoulders off the floor, and rest your hands on the cushion – don't cling on to it for dear life!
Repeat 5 times

Exercise 9: for inside legs
Lying flat on the floor, turn the legs outwards from the hips and place the cushion between your heels and squeeze them together. Hold for a count of 10.
Repeat 5 times

Exercises with a partner
Before you start, make sure
that your partner realises
that the key to Body Control
is relaxing into a position,
not being forced into it.

Exercise 10
Lie on your back with your
knees together and bent in
towards your chest. Your
partner then presses your
knees gently down,
stretching out your lower
spine.
*Repeat 4 times,
alternating with Exercise 11*

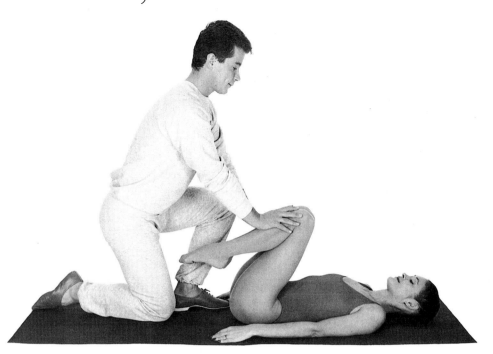

**Exercise 11: for your inner
thighs**
Lie on your back with your
legs straight up in the air.
Your partner then holds your
feet and opens your legs as
wide as they will comfortably
go, and then brings them
back together and crosses
them over.
The hardest part of this
exercise is trying not to
giggle.

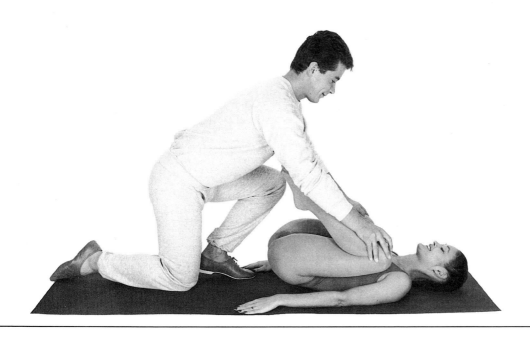

Exercise 12
This exercise can be done either alone
or with a partner.
Sit with your knees bent, your feet
about 12 inches apart, your back
straight and your hands on knees with
your elbows bent.
Round your spine, leaning backwards
until your arms are almost straight.
Then pull up, straightening and
stretching your spine with your head
back and your upper chest open. You
should feel the stretch right down your
back.
Repeat 5 times

In the second version, your partner
pushes your head gently forward, to
help you round your spine, then with a
cushion to stop his knees digging into
your back, *gently* pulls your head up
and back to stretch your spine.
Repeat 5 times

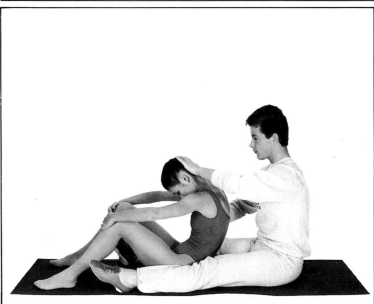

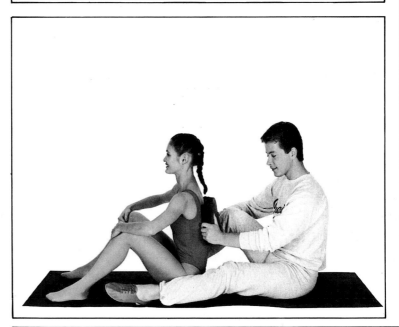
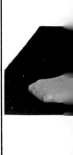

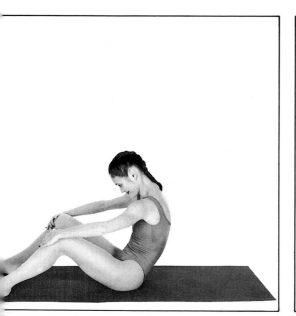

Exercise 13: for your sides and waist
Lie on your left side, with your left leg bent under you, and your left hand on your right hip. Your partner holds your right ankle with his right hand, and takes your right hand in his left.

As he slowly pulls you up, keep your left hand on your right hip. Then allow your partner to lower you slowly to the floor. *Repeat 5 times on each side*
On the final repeat, come up higher. Release the left hand

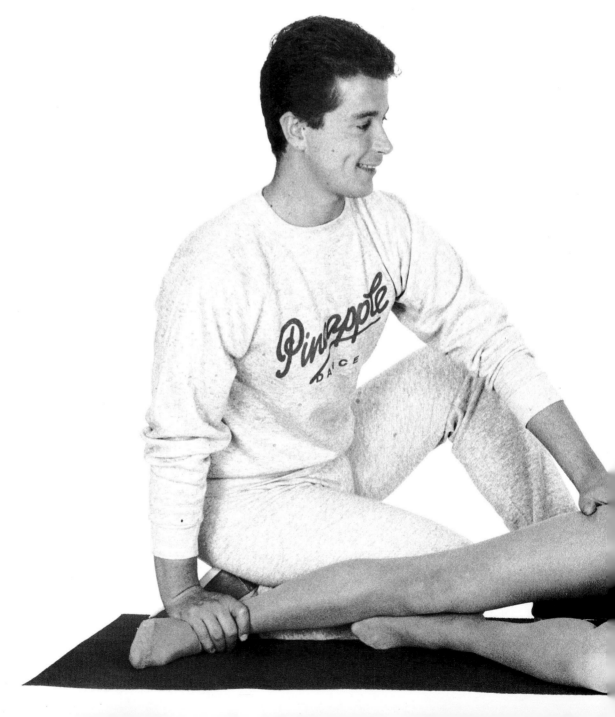

and then the right, pulling out and away. Hold the
unsupported position for a count of 5, then lower yourself
slowly to the floor.
Repeat the whole sequence twice on each side

Sandy Strallen
STRETCH 'N' TONE

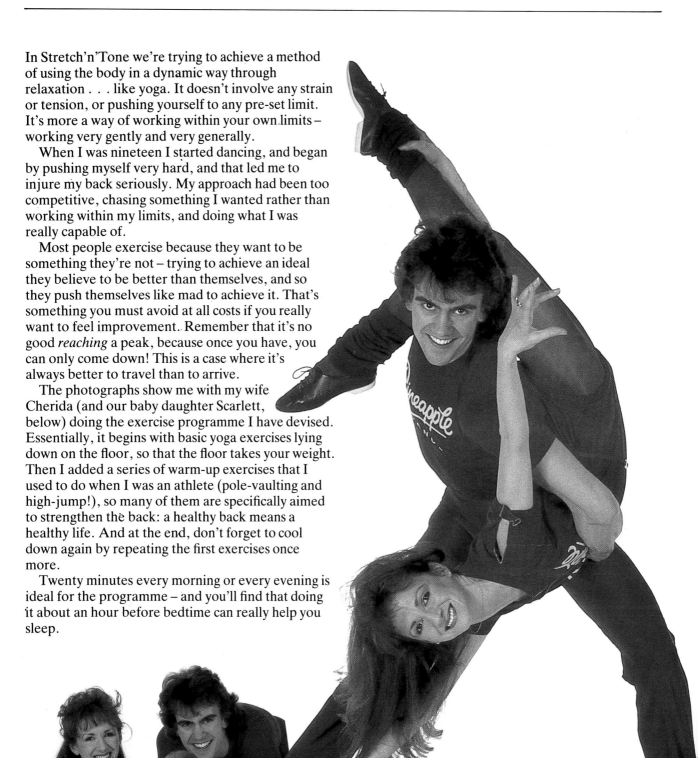

In Stretch'n'Tone we're trying to achieve a method of using the body in a dynamic way through relaxation . . . like yoga. It doesn't involve any strain or tension, or pushing yourself to any pre-set limit. It's more a way of working within your own limits – working very gently and very generally.

When I was nineteen I started dancing, and began by pushing myself very hard, and that led me to injure my back seriously. My approach had been too competitive, chasing something I wanted rather than working within my limits, and doing what I was really capable of.

Most people exercise because they want to be something they're not – trying to achieve an ideal they believe to be better than themselves, and so they push themselves like mad to achieve it. That's something you must avoid at all costs if you really want to feel improvement. Remember that it's no good *reaching* a peak, because once you have, you can only come down! This is a case where it's always better to travel than to arrive.

The photographs show me with my wife Cherida (and our baby daughter Scarlett, below) doing the exercise programme I have devised. Essentially, it begins with basic yoga exercises lying down on the floor, so that the floor takes your weight. Then I added a series of warm-up exercises that I used to do when I was an athlete (pole-vaulting and high-jump!), so many of them are specifically aimed to strengthen the back: a healthy back means a healthy life. And at the end, don't forget to cool down again by repeating the first exercises once more.

Twenty minutes every morning or every evening is ideal for the programme – and you'll find that doing it about an hour before bedtime can really help you sleep.

Exercise 1
Lie flat on your back, your arms by your sides and your lower spine pushed well into the floor.
Swing your arms over your head, flex your feet and stretch out as hard as you can, so that your heels come off the floor. Relax.
Repeat 4 times

Exercise 2
Sit on your heels with your back straight. Let your head drop forward so that you stretch the back of your neck and your upper spine. Return to your starting position, then let your head drop back, squeezing your shoulder blades together, so that your upper chest is open. Return to your starting position.
Repeat 4 times

Exercise 3
Crouch down on your toes with your palms flat on the floor, and your head tucked under. Leaving your hands and feet where they are, raise and lower your bottom three times, keeping your knees slightly bent, then straighten your legs. If you can't straighten them completely, go as far as you comfortably can.
Repeat 8 times

Exercise 4
From the same starting position as Exercise 3 (1), stretch your right leg out behind you and with your head up (2), bounce gently, stretching the leg, eight times. Return to your starting position and repeat with your left leg.
Repeat the whole exercise 4 times

Return to your starting position, then straighten your legs (3), and slowly roll up (4), one vertebra at a time (5), until you're standing with your back straight, your stomach pulled in, your chin parallel with the floor (6). Check your posture in the mirror.

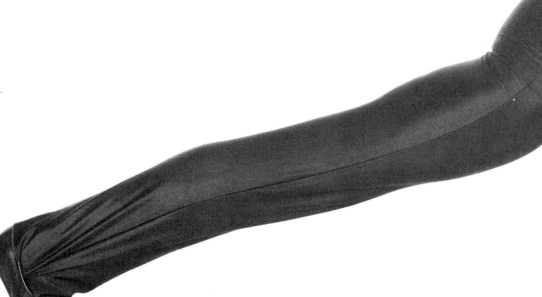

Exercise 5
Stand with your feet about 18 inches apart and parallel, your arms above your head. Stretch up as hard as you can with your left arm, at the same time bending your left knee. You should feel the stretch right down your left side. Return to your starting position, and stretch up to the right.
Repeat 8 times

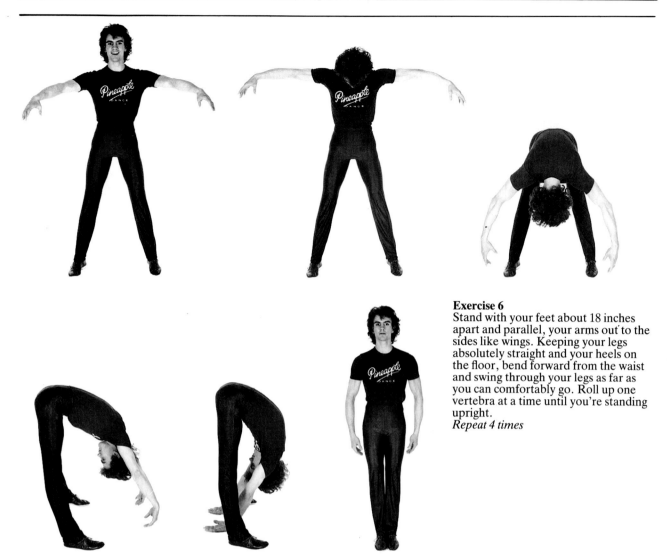

Exercise 6
Stand with your feet about 18 inches apart and parallel, your arms out to the sides like wings. Keeping your legs absolutely straight and your heels on the floor, bend forward from the waist and swing through your legs as far as you can comfortably go. Roll up one vertebra at a time until you're standing upright.
Repeat 4 times

Exercise 7
Stand with your feet about 18 inches apart and pointing outwards. Keeping your trunk square on to the front, swing your left arm over your head and out to the right. You should feel the stretch right down to your left side. Return to your starting position, and stretch over to the right.
Repeat 8 times

Exercise 8
Stand with your feet about 18 inches apart and parallel, your arms straight out to the sides. Twisting from the waist, swing your right hand down to your left foot, putting the palm of your left hand flat on the floor if you can, and your left arm straight up in the air.

Return to your starting position, and then swing down to the other side.
Repeat 4 times
Repeat the exercise, bending your left knee as you swing down to your left foot, and vice versa.
Repeat 4 times

Exercise 9
With your back straight and your arms held out in front of you, slowly bend your knees. When you are virtually sitting on your heels, sink back onto the floor, hugging your knees, then – keeping them bent for as long as possible – roll slowly backwards, one vertebra at a time, until you're lying flat on the floor.

Raise your head and shoulders, and slowly roll up again, keeping your lower spine pressed into the floor as long as possible (you should feel the pull in your stomach muscles, *not* in your back). Stretch forward over your legs as far as you can go, then, returning to a sitting position, flex your feet and roll slowly down again.
Repeat from photograph eight 4 times

Exercise 10

Stand with your feet together and parallel, arms by your sides. Bend forward from the waist, then bend your knees until you are crouching down. Put your knees on the floor, and stretch your hands out in front of you as far as they will go. Arching your back like a cat, push your chest forward until your arms bend, and you wind up lying flat on the floor. Push your trunk up by straightening your arms, and tilting your head back. Then bend your knees and push your bottom up, arching your back again. Sit back on your heels and straighten up. Return to your starting position.
Repeat 4 times

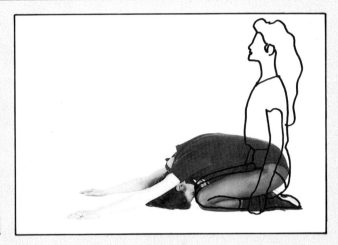

Exercise 11
Sit, pressing the soles of your feet together, with your knees as far apart as they will comfortably go. Curve your spine, and bounce gently forward from the waist 8 times. Return to your starting position, and repeat with your back straight.
Repeat 4 times

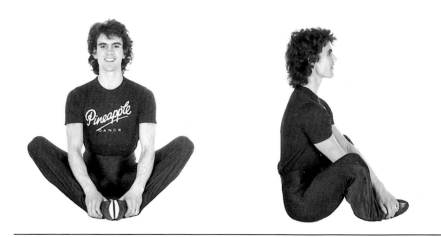

Exercise 12
Sit with your right leg stretched out in front of you, your left leg bent and your left foot as close to your body as possible. Point your right foot, hold on to your right ankle and bounce forward, with your spine curved, 8 times. Repeat with a straight back and your right foot flexed.
Repeat whole exercise 4 times each side

Exercise 13
Sit with your legs crossed and your back straight. Put your right arm over your right shoulder, and grab the fingers of your left hand (if you can't quite reach, lay your hands flat on your back as close together as possible). Bend as far forward over your legs as you can.
Repeat 4 times

Exercise 14
Sit cross-legged, and circle your shoulders by rolling them down and forward, lifting them up as high as you can (try and touch your ears), then dropping them back and down.
Repeat 8 times

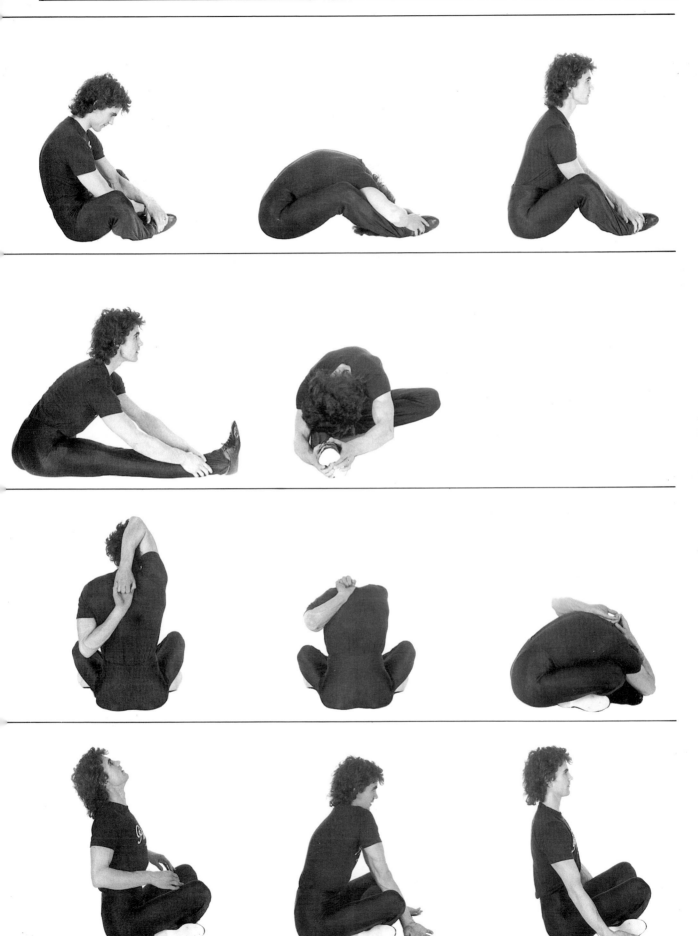

Exercise 15
Kneel with your thighs pressed tightly
together, and your arms straight out in
front of you. Keeping your body
absolutely straight from your knees to
the top of your head, lean back. You
should feel the pull down the front of
your thighs. Return to your starting
position, then sink back onto your
heels, head up, arching your spine
(left). Then bend forward over your
thighs, stretching your spine out, then
sit back up, before returning to your
starting position.
Repeat 4 times

Exercise 16
Stand with your feet about 18 inches apart, and parallel, with your arms raised above your head. Swing forward, bending your knees, then as your fingertips brush the floor, straighten them again as your arms continue swinging back and up. Swing back into your starting position, bending your knees as your fingers brush the floor. *Repeat 8 times*

Exercise 17
Stand with your feet together, your arms by your sides. Walk on the spot pressing down on each foot alternately, making sure your toes don't actually come off the ground (4 times)

then lift your toes just a few inches off the floor (4 times) and finally, lift your feet about 12 inches off the floor, so that you are jogging on the spot, knees up, toes pointed.
Repeat 8 times

Exercise 18
Stand with your feet together and parallel. Put your right leg straight out behind you, your right arm out in front of you, making a straight line, bend your left knee and put your left arm out behind you. As you jump changè position in mid air, so that you land with your left leg out behind you and your right knee bent.
Repeat 16 times

Exercise 19
Put your right leg and left arm out in front of you, parallel to the floor. Bounce once on your left foot, then change arms and legs in mid air, and carry on alternating right and left, bouncing once on both feet between changes.
Repeat 16 times

Exercise 20
Star jumps: start with your feet together, arms by your sides, then bend your knees and as you jump your feet apart, swing your arms up over your head, clapping as you do so. Jump your feet together again, bending your knees as you land.
Repeat 16 times

Cool-down
To complete the programme, repeat exercises 1 to 4, in the reverse order, in order to cool down properly.

SOUL JAZZ

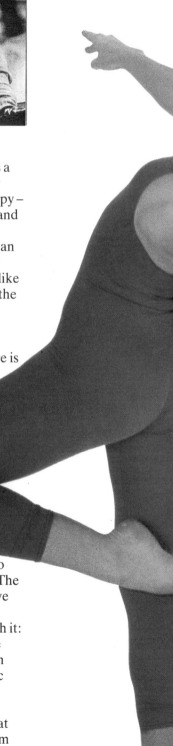

When I put together my own dance company, Maasai, a couple of years ago, what I wanted was a group whose style was unique. In soul jazz, every teacher has his or her own style, and mine is snappy – it has more bite, more edge – it's very American and has the feel of American black music. In fact, for rhythm, there's still no better jazz dance music than Duke Ellington's. In my choreography and in my classes it is rare that we do anything slow: what I like is high energy and speed, but you mustn't follow the exercises here too fast to start with as they are devised for students who have a decent ballet training, and ideally they should be learned in a class. When trying them at home, remember there is a warm-up section of stretches and bends to be done before you attempt any of the travelling steps, and stick to these if it's getting too difficult.

Although I trained in ballet and tap, and once had my own ballet school, most of my work these days is with professional dancers and choreography for Massai. The two dancers pictured here are Oké, who has been training with me for about a year, and Helen, who came to me from the Dance Theatre of London. The routine they are demonstrating is something I have been working on recently.

What is most important is the way you approach it: the way you learn has to be clean. Take your time and do it correctly. And don't try the combination without doing the warm-up first. Put on any music you like – fast or slow – and do it for your own pleasure. (Don't try doing it to music you can't enjoy!) You can count with any music . . . the beat doesn't matter. Learn the steps first, then put them to the music.

Warm-up

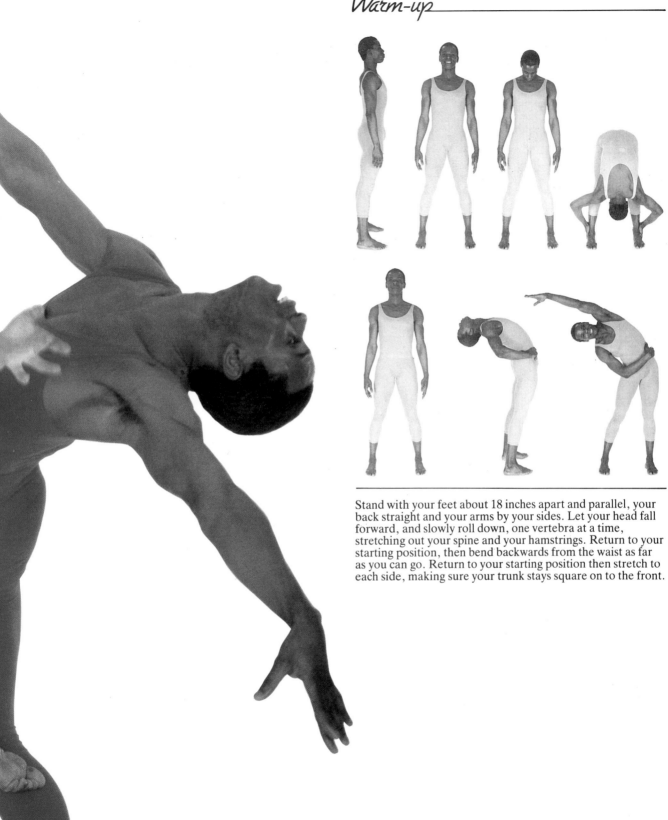

Stand with your feet about 18 inches apart and parallel, your back straight and your arms by your sides. Let your head fall forward, and slowly roll down, one vertebra at a time, stretching out your spine and your hamstrings. Return to your starting position, then bend backwards from the waist as far as you can go. Return to your starting position then stretch to each side, making sure your trunk stays square on to the front.

139

Pliés
Knee bends

Exercise 1
(1) Stand with your feet together, pointing outwards, arms curved in at hip level in front of you. (2) Raise your arms in front of you, then stretch them out at shoulder height (3). Bend your knees till they are directly over your toes (4), straighten up and repeat. Then bend as low as you can bringing your

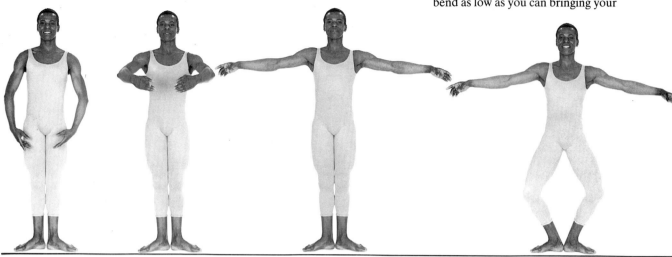

Exercise 2
Stand with your feet about 18 inches apart, pointing outwards, and your arms out to the sides at shoulder level.

Repeat as for Exercise 1, keeping your heels on the floor throughout during the pliés.

Exercise 3
Stand with your right foot about 8 inches in front of your left, both feet pointing outwards, and your arms out to the sides at shoulder level. Repeat as for Exercise 1.

Exercise 4 (not illustrated)
Stand with your right foot directly in front of the left, both feet pointing as far out to the sides as possible, and repeat as for Exercise 1.

arms down, keeping your back straight, so that your heels come off the floor (5), straighten up and repeat. Return to position (6), and go up on your toes, bringing your arms down at the same time (7), then straight up over your head (8) and (9), finishing with them at your sides as you come down.

Stretch

Exercise 5
Stand with your feet about 18 inches apart, and parallel, with your arms above your head. Keeping your trunk square on to the front, stretch over to the right, then twisting at the waist, and keeping your back absolutely flat, swing across to the left, stretch up and return to your starting position.
Repeat to the other side

Tendues

Footwork

Exercise 6
Stand with your feet together and parallel, arms by your sides. Point your right foot and stretch it out in front of you, keeping your toe on the floor. Bring it back to your starting position.
Repeat 8 times with each foot.
With your heels together, feet pointing outwards, repeat the exercise, stretching out to the sides.
Repeat 8 times with each foot.

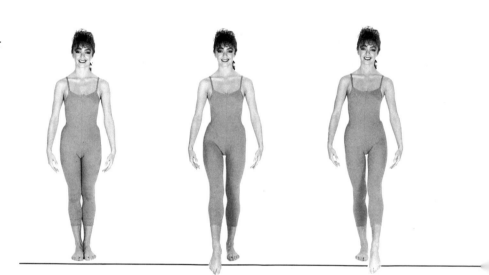

Battements

Legwork

Exercise 8
Repeat as for Exercise 6, only this time stretch your arms out to the sides, and bring your leg up, parallel to the floor. As you swing your leg up, you should feel the stretch in your hamstrings and the muscles at the back of your knees, but not in the muscles at the front of your thighs.
Repeat 8 times with each leg

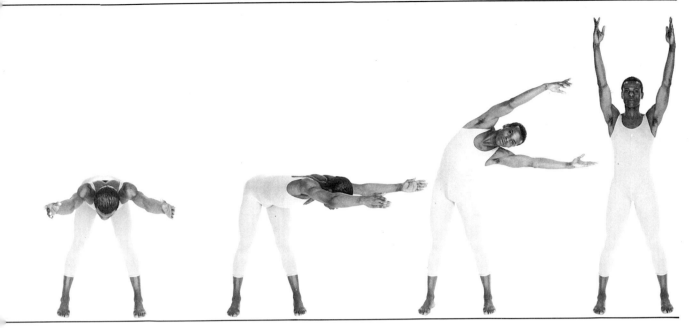

Exercise 7
Repeat as for Exercise 6, only lift your
pointed toe a few inches off the ground.
Repeat 8 times with each foot

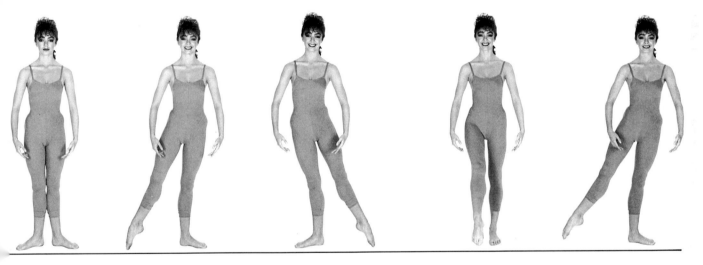

Floorwork

Exercise 9
Sit with the soles of your feet together, your knees as wide apart as they'll go, and your back straight. Curve your spine, and bend as far forward as you can go. Bounce gently 8 times.

Exercise 11
Sit with your legs stretched as far apart as they will go, your feet pointed and your arms out to the sides. Curve your spine and bounce gently forward 8 times. Repeat with your back straight and your feet flexed.

Exercise 12
Sit in the same position as for Exercise 11. Keeping your trunk square on to the front, stretch over to the left and bounce gently 8 times.
Repeat to the right
Flex your feet and twisting at the waist (make sure your bottom stays firmly on the floor) reach across to your right foot with your left arm. Hold for a count of 8.
Repeat to the left

Exercise 13
Lie flat on your back, legs stretched out. Take hold of your right knee and pull it into your chest. Then grab your foot and stretch your leg out over your head as far as it will go.
Repeat with your left leg

Exercise 10
Sit with your arms and legs straight out in front of you, your feet pointed and your back straight. Curve your spine, and bounce gently forward 8 times. Repeat with your back straight and your feet flexed.

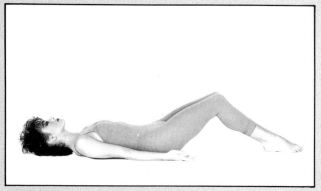

Exercise 14
Lie flat on the floor, your knees up, and your palms facing upwards. Sit up over a count of 4, stretch your arms out in front of you at shoulder height, then twist to the right,

keeping your bottom on the floor, and hold for a count of ten. Return to the centre over a count of 4.
Repeat to the left

Exercise 15
Repeat Exercise 15 with your right leg stretched up into the air.
Repeat to the left

Exercise 16 (left)
Repeat with both legs stretched up into the air. Obviously this requires very good balance!

Isolations

Exercise 17
Stand with your feet about 18 inches apart, and parallel, the palms of your hands flat on your stomach. Push your chest forward, then pull it back, caving it in, keeping your arms and shoulders as still as you can. Then, keeping your hips and legs absolutely still, and your shoulders parallel to the floor, move your trunk to the right, back to the centre, then out to the left. You can also do this exercise in a circle – trunk left, back, right, forward.
Repeat 4 times

Exercise 18
Stand with your feet about 18 inches apart and parallel, your elbows into your waist, and your hands out. Swing your left hip up to touch your left elbow, back to the centre, and repeat to the right. Push your pelvis forward, back to the centre, then push your bottom out.
Repeat 4 times

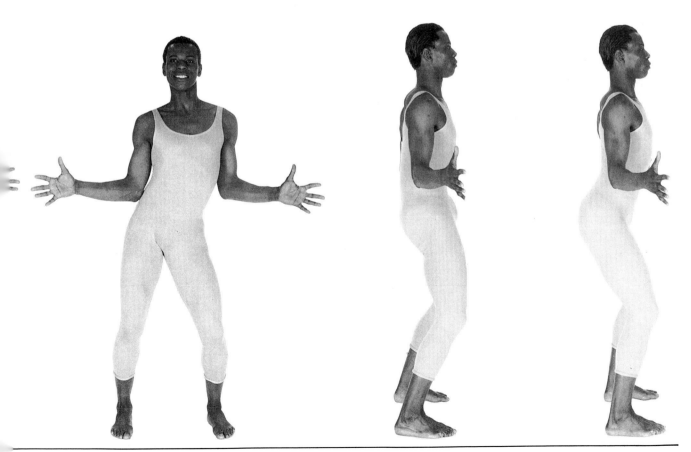

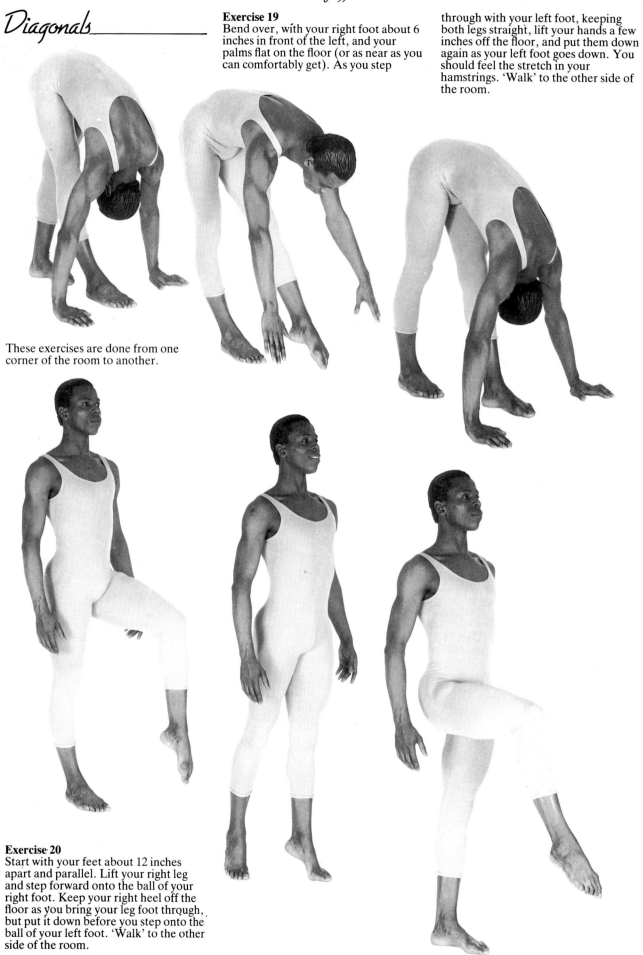

Diagonals

Exercise 19
Bend over, with your right foot about 6 inches in front of the left, and your palms flat on the floor (or as near as you can comfortably get). As you step through with your left foot, keeping both legs straight, lift your hands a few inches off the floor, and put them down again as your left foot goes down. You should feel the stretch in your hamstrings. 'Walk' to the other side of the room.

These exercises are done from one corner of the room to another.

Exercise 20
Start with your feet about 12 inches apart and parallel. Lift your right leg and step forward onto the ball of your right foot. Keep your right heel off the floor as you bring your leg foot through, but put it down before you step onto the ball of your left foot. 'Walk' to the other side of the room.

Exercise 21
Step forward with your right foot, then
with your left. Bring your right foot up
to join the left, and jump on the spot,
with your legs together. 'Walk' to the
other side of the room.

Exercise 22
Stand with your feet together
and parallel, arms out to the
sides. Bending your knees,
step forward onto your right
foot, and then, as you kick
your left leg as high as you
can, straighten both legs.
'Walk' across the room,
kicking with alternate legs.
First kick to the front then
repeat the exercise kicking to
the side.

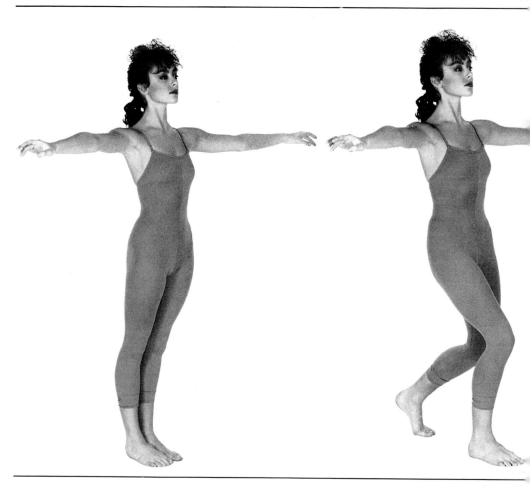

Routine

(A) Start with your left foot extended in front of your right leg, which is bent, both feet pointing outwards, your arms extended in front. (B) Put your weight on the ball of your left foot, and bring your right foot into your left knee, stretching your right arm up and your left arm out to the side. (C) Bend from the waist to the right, pulling your right elbow in to your body, and (D) swing your right leg across in front of your left (E). Straighten up, and step across to the left with your left leg (F), point your foot, and with a small jumping movement transfer your weight from one foot to the other (G). Then raise and point your right foot, and bring it round in front of your left, so that you are ready to repeat the routine, starting on your right foot (H).

Port de Bras
Arms

Exercise 23
Stand with your feet together and parallel, your arms by your sides. Raise your arms to shoulder height twice, then above your head twice.

Exercise 24
Extend your left leg and left arm out to the side, bend your right knee and stretch your right arm up into the air, Repeat the other side.
Repeat once each side

Exercise 25
Stand with your feet about 18 inches apart and parallel, your arms stretched out to the sides. Keeping your hips square on to the front, twist to the right from the waist, swing your left arm over

to the right. Bend your left knee, and shift your weight onto it. Straighten up, return to your starting position, and repeat to the left.
Repeat once each side

Exercise 26
Stand with your feet about 18 inches apart, arms curved above your head. Keeping your hips square on to the front, twist to the left, stretching your right arm over to the left, and putting your left hand on your hip. Raise your left arm into the air, then bend backwards as far as you can go, stretching both arms out as hard as you can. Return to your starting position and repeat the other side.
Repeat once each side

Acknowledgements

We would particularly like to acknowledge the photographic talents of Jeremy Enness, who was responsible for photographing all the exercise classes in Part 3, and indeed for many of the other photographs that appear in this book. Individual credits are as follows: Catherine Ashmore: 24; Associated Newspapers: 9; Mike Bailey: 30 (top and below), 31 (bottom left), 63 (top), 158; BBC Hulton Picture Library: 36, 37 (bottom), 40 (left), 48 (right); Anthony Crickmay: 18; Donald Cooper 7 (below left); Dominic Photography: 19, 33; Jeremy Enness: 2/3, 12 (top right, centre left, bottom left), 15, 16, 17, 20/21, 26, 27, 34/35, 37 (top), 43, 44/45, 47, 48 (right), 52, 53, 54/55, 56, 60, 75, 78-157; Jill Furmanovsky: 42; John Gordon: 42; Chris Harris: 25; Kobal Collection: 26 (below), 28, 32, 37 (bottom); London Features International: 29; The Marketing Office: 7 (centre and below right); Brendan Monks: 31 (top and bottom right); Barbara Morgan: 22; Chris Nash: 12 (bottom right), 13 (below), 23 (below), 38, 40, 50 (right), 65, 70, 73; Press Association: 11 (left); Rex Features: 49 (right); Steve Sandon: 11 (right); John Robinson: 15; Stephen Rumney: 50 (left), 51; Summerton Burton Management: 16, 94; John Swannell: 1, 59, 76, 160.

Further information on classes and publications mentioned in this book is available from:

Pineapple Dance Studios
7 Langley Street
Covent Garden
London WC2

Pineapple West Dance Studios
60 Paddington Street
London W1